African Minds Higher Education Dynamics Series Vol. 5

Revisiting Africa's Flagship Universities

Local, National and International Dynamics

James Ransom

AFRICAN MINDS

First published in 2024 by African Minds
4 Eccleston Place, Somerset West 7130, Cape Town, South Africa
info@africanminds.org.za
www.africanminds.org.za

ISBN (paper): 978–1-928502–95-1
eBook edition: 978–1-928502–98-2
ePub edition: 978–1-928502–97-5

ORDERS:
African Minds
4 Eccleston Place, Somerset West 7130, Cape Town, South Africa
info@africanminds.org.za
www.africanminds.org.za

For orders from outside Africa:
African Books Collective
PO Box 721, Oxford OX1 9EN, UK
orders@africanbookscollective.com

CONTENTS

LIST OF TABLES AND FIGURES

ACKNOWLEDGEMENTS

Thank you to Professor Tristan McCowan and Dr Vincent Carpentier at UCL, and Dr Vincent Manirakiza at the University of Rwanda, for sharing your academic wisdom. Thank you to UCL, the Sir Richard Stapley Educational Trust and Universities UK for financial support. Thank you to African Minds and the peer reviewers for your time and guidance in publishing this book. And thank you to my family for supporting me.

FOREWORD

James Ransom and I met for the first time in 2010 in Cape Town, South Africa, at the Conference of Executive Heads of the Association of Commonwealth Universities (ACU), the theme of which was 'Universities and the Millennium Development Goals'. James was then working with the ACU, and I was attending as secretary general of the Association of African Universities. After the conference, we went our separate ways but both of us maintained our interest in higher education, whether at national, regional, or international level. Fourteen years later, this book on engagement of universities in Africa has brought us together again.

In the mid-20th century, it was well established that the three missions of a university were teaching, research, and community service or outreach, the latter being understood as providing services or reaching out to the community, essentially a one-way process. By the end of the 20th century, perhaps in light of the criticism levelled at universities for being ivory towers and not contributing to national development, the notion of universities engaging with society emerged. What such engagement meant, and how it should be undertaken, was not clear.

In an attempt to explore the issue and better understand university engagement, the ACU initiated a research project in 2000. A year later, it launched a survey among its 500 member universities in the Commonwealth of the former British Empire using an extensive consultation document entitled 'Engagement as a Core Value for the University'. The document provided a definition of engagement as follows:

> *Strenuous, thoughtful, argumentative interaction with the non-university world in at least four spheres: setting universities' aims, purposes, and priorities; relating teaching and learning to the wider world; the back-and-forth dialogue between researchers and practitioners; and taking on wider responsibilities as neighbours and citizens. (Bjarnason and Coldstream, 2003, p. 25)*

The outcome was a book published in 2003, titled *The Idea of Engagement: Universities in Society*, in which thirteen senior academics from five Commonwealth countries, drawing from the results of the survey, gave their perspectives on the engagement debate. The book concludes that, to meet the demands of government, industry and the world of work, society and the community 'requires a university to be fully engaged, not tacitly but explicitly, and not only in research partnerships but in ways that profoundly influence both teaching and research as well as reaching out to meet societies' intellectual, social and cultural needs' (Bjarnason and Coldstream, 2003, p. xii).

In Africa, I cannot think of a better example than the University for Development Studies (UDS) in Tamale in the north of Ghana to illustrate how a university fully engages with its community for development purposes. Created in 1992 as a public university, a major objective of UDS is to 'blend the academic world with that of the community in order to provide constructive interaction between the two for the total development of northern Ghana in particular, and the country as a whole' (UDS, 2024). The university has a pro-poor focus and aims at playing an active role in addressing societal problems, especially in rural areas, for speedy development. A unique feature of the university is that every student, each year, must spend the third semester undertaking community-based field practical works.

In this book, Ransom explores ten flagship Anglophone universities in sub-Saharan Africa to understand how these institutions engage with and contribute to the development of their local surroundings and at the same time respond to regional and global development agendas. And he does that by analysing their strategic plans to get an insight into their institutional priorities and values and their engagement practices with their communities, their governments, the cities where they are located and their international partners.

As pointed out by the author, any analysis of the development role of universities in Africa needs to be historically situated. The so-called flagship universities in this book, and in other similar literature, are essentially what one might call 'first-generation' public universities in Africa. In each country they were the first, or among the first, higher education institutions to be set up, for many, at the time of independence. Their academic structure, governance model, course curricula, and language and methods of instruction were all modelled on European universities with which they developed strong ties. They were often staffed by European academics supporting the African ones who were trained in Europe. They were created in major cities, meant for the elite in African societies, and alienated from rural areas where most of the population live and where the development challenges are greatest. The relevance of such higher education institutions to Africa's post-independence development has often been questioned.

These universities thrived for a couple of decades with generous funding from the North. Then, over the next two decades, they faced serious budget cuts resulting not only from the downturn of African economies but also from the misguided policy of several international funders and donors that funding basic and secondary education, instead of higher education, yielded greater economic and social returns. The situation worsened with political turmoil in African countries in which these universities invariably became involved. Battered, the universities nevertheless weathered all the storms and proved to be remarkably resilient.

As shown in this book, these first-generation universities have now evolved into institutions that are nationally and regionally recognised as centres of learning and research and are pivotal actors in shaping national policies, fostering innovation, and addressing pressing societal challenges. But they still have to address two thorny issues: first, achieving financial sustainability and reducing graduate unemployment. Second, their persistence in following higher education trends in the North, irrespective of their relevance to the local context, is questionable. They may also need to reconsider their aspiration to be world-class universities or to be globally ranked, which many African academics consider futile and inappropriate.

A characteristic inherited by most flagship universities as a result of their history is their weak partnerships with other African universities. By comparison, they have a far greater number of partnerships with universities in the North. Individual African universities lack resources to address some of the real development challenges of the continent. However, by collaborating with other universities in the region and by pooling their resources, they can overcome their shortcomings. Over the past decade several networks and collaborative projects involving African universities have been created to encourage greater regional collaboration. But this is still work in progress and more needs to be done by the individual universities themselves.

By unpacking the complexities of African development and the role of universities within it, this book provides invaluable knowledge for policymakers, university leaders, and development practitioners alike. This work challenges us to think differently about African flagship universities. More importantly, it provides the tools to turn that thinking into action, offering a valuable resource for anyone invested in the future of African higher education. Perhaps the most compelling argument for reading this book is encapsulated in a key insight by the author: to understand the potential of higher education in development in Africa, we need to better understand Africa's flagship universities.

Professor Goolam Mohamedbhai
Former secretary general of the Association of African Universities
Former president of the International Association of Universities
Former vice chancellor of the University of Mauritius
Mauritius, September 2024

PROLOGUE

It is 2021 and I am a research affiliate at the University of Rwanda, meeting academics, staff and policymakers, and gathering information, some of which will later inform this book. There are nine campuses, of which three (including the headquarters) are in the capital and largest city, Kigali, and I am on a mission to spend time at them all.

The College of Medicine and Health Sciences sits off a busy road in Remera, towards Kigali International Airport and east of the city centre. The campus was once the Kigali Institute of Education, and then the Kigali Health Institute, before the creation of the University of Rwanda in 2013. I surrender my passport to the security guard, and enter the leafy campus – it is spotless and quiet, with a gentle breeze bringing the sounds from a nearby school.

I am here to learn about health outreach at the College. Outreach is embedded into courses within several schools, including dentistry, public health, and nursing and midwifery. Whereas research and teaching were hit by COVID lockdowns, outreach activity increased, in particular where students and staff provide health services to the community.

Outreach work takes place throughout the country and the community in question changes: sometimes a neighbourhood close to the campus or on the outskirts of the city, sometimes it can be five hours away in a rural area. Visits are usually for one week each year ("but actually, one week probably is not enough", noted one lecturer). Before staff and students go to the community, they get statistics from community health workers about common issues. These workers sit under the Ministry of Health, but are unpaid volunteers. Students are then at the centre of activities throughout the visit.

Health outreach has limited funding, drawn from the University of Rwanda budget. Additional funding would allow the university to visit these sites two or three times a year, and track progress, measure impact, and capture issues. The small budget does not currently allow any evaluation. There is also a lack of connectivity between the government institutions whose work is supported by the health outreach activity of the university, other stakeholders who might also contribute (such as NGOs), the community, and the university.

Despite these issues, bridging the field and the classroom proves valuable. "Whenever we go to the community, it really pays off because we find, in many cases, some of the issues we could not even have imagined that they still exist", observed one member of staff.

A twenty-minute drive brings me to the College of Science and Technology, formerly the Kigali Institute of Science and Technology (and before that, a military base). Again I surrender my passport at the gate. The campus is sprawling and very green, running behind the Kigali Serena Hotel, a short walk south of the city centre. Students walk to lectures; I check the map on my phone for the location of my next meeting – there are no campus maps.

I am here to learn about projects the College is involved with in Kigali. These are often discrete, defined projects led by the City of Kigali. These include running and moderating a design competition for public benches that reimagine public spaces post-COVID, with designs submitted by students, and a city water resilience assessment where graduates from relevant programmes are invited to workshops to find solutions to manage storm water and waste water, with potential job opportunities for students. Sometimes these city-led initiatives are channeled by city officials to university staff where there is a personal connection; for larger projects or where public money is involved, initiatives tend to involve a public tendering process.

Other projects are organised by the university, in collaboration with the City of Kigali. One example is a workshop with the community on informal housing. These events are carefully designed and delivered, with around 200 community members attending. Discussions are also deliberately framed: "not the typical, 'what challenges do you have, how can we solve them?' but trying to understand, what are the qualities that these people need in housing? How do they understand housing? How do they appreciate space? How much space is enough for these communities?", explained an academic.

The workshop drew on the internal school budget to provide a lunch and was hosted on *Umuganda* (a community work morning on the last Saturday of every month), so members of the university did some cleaning together first with the community to break the ice. Small group sessions then used physical props to understand layout and space in housing – asking, 'Where would you put the bedroom, and how large does it need to be? Why?'. 'What type of window would you prefer? Why?'. This uncovered some interesting insights, such as a preference for outside hand basins to encourage hygiene and public health – a preference that pre-dated COVID. "In the end, I have this nice picture of what your aspirations are," added the lecturer.

Although previous academic studies have shed light on the battle between two polarised perceptions of the flagship university – a great national institution driving growth and development, or a beleaguered, near-bankrupt monolith outmanoeuvred by newer, more nimble competitors – none in doing so illuminate the role of flagships in their local area, and the sort of local engagement activity I encountered at the University of Rwanda. This book revisits Africa's flagship universities and their local, national and international roles. The University of Rwanda is joined by nine other flagships spanning Ethiopia, Ghana, Mauritius, Namibia, Nigeria, South Africa, Uganda, Zambia, and Zimbabwe. By using – and critiquing – strategic planning documents, the voice of African flagship universities is at the forefront of the analysis.

The breadth of engagement activity I witnessed is only part of the University of Rwanda's role in places such as Kigali, and only part of the role of the university in national development. By exploring the balance between national imperatives and local and international engagement, this book seeks to offer a nuanced perspective on how these institutions contribute to development. I argue that flagship universities can be important actors in shaping and delivering policy and planning within African societies. But above all, I believe that to understand the potential of higher education in development, we need to better understand flagship universities.

CHAPTER 1

INTRODUCTION

Despite growing interest in the role of higher education in development, there is limited analysis of how universities engage with and contribute to the development of their local surroundings, particularly in sub-Saharan Africa. This book examines the roles and activities of flagship universities in addressing development challenges in African city regions. In turn, it generates new knowledge on the traits of public universities in Africa, the challenges and opportunities facing these institutions, and practices of local engagement.

Flagship universities are often the most prestigious and largest higher education institutions in their country, and wield considerable influence (Teferra, 2017, p. 2). They are spaces for shaping public discourse, and are historically linked to advancing national development (Lebeau, 2008). This book seeks to answer a seemingly straightforward question: are flagship universities in African city regions developing a local focus alongside their historic national mission? There are several reasons why such a shift may take place, all of which suggest a greater role for public institutions based in urban areas. First, the challenges and opportunities of urbanisation are especially acute in African cities (Parnell and Pieterse, 2014). Second, there has been a wider push for cities to take on a range of new roles: to help meet the UN Sustainable Development Goals (Moreira da Silva and Kamal-Chaoui, 2019), to tackle grand challenges (Acuto, 2016), and to contribute to global governance and improve international relations (Curtis, 2014; Herrschel and Newman, 2017). This is partly driven by the popular notion of 'resilience', which shifts the onus of (and responsibility for) tackling development challenges from nations to cities (Vale, 2014). Third, there is a recognition that universities in the Global North are being called upon to contribute more to their place and their locality (Birch, Perry and Taylor, 2013; Pugh et al., 2016), to engage beyond teaching and research (Nelles and Vorley, 2010), to tailor their teaching and research to the area (Goddard et al., 2016), and to leverage their international connections for local benefit (Addie, 2016). There has been little work to test whether a similar 'local turn' is taking place in universities in the Global South.

The contribution that universities and, separately, cities can make to global development has become a focus of academic and policy attention, with both universities and cities at risk of being seen as a panacea and saddled with unrealistic expectations. This book sits between two active, but mostly separate, research areas: universities and development, and universities and their local role. The literature on universities and local development is largely written from a Northern perspective and uses European or US case studies, although an African exception is South Africa, with a recent flurry of work (Bank, Cloete and van Schalkwyk (2018) and van

Schalkwyk and de Lange (2018), for example). In closely related fields such as community engagement, a similar pattern emerges, with most of the theories and concepts imported from the Global North (Fongwa et al., 2022, p. 3). As such, this book also contributes to broader scholarship on African higher education, a field experiencing a recent rise with new research communities beginning to emerge outside of South Africa, the home of most existing work (Lebeau, 2020, p. 447; Zavale and Schneijderberg, 2022, p. 199).

The two major studies of African flagship universities (Teferra, 2017; Cloete, Bunting and van Schalkwyk, 2018) provide a valuable academic foundation, but do not focus on the local (that is, sub-national) development role of these institutions. This book addresses this gap, looking specifically at engagement with communities, government, city hall and others in local areas. It also revisits the concept of the flagship university, expanding the analysis to include several institutions not previously included in multi-country studies, and introduces a new lens for exploring priorities, plans and values – the university strategic plan. In doing so, this study identifies the distinctive traits of modern flagship universities, and their role in the development of sub-Saharan African city regions. At the same time, it helps to address the paucity of work on local university engagement in Africa, contributing a multi-country analysis to a field dominated by single-country studies, and does so using a multi-scalar approach that emphasises the local, national and international dimensions of university activity.[1] Our understanding of the challenges and incentives of engagement is deepened, and these are set within broader frameworks of the role of universities in society, their historical origins, and their relationships with government.

University activity aimed at increasing local engagement – including that concerned with industry partnerships and technology transfer – has often been grouped together under the banner of 'third mission activity', as distinct from 'core' research and teaching activity. Nelles and Vorley (2010, p. 342) cite several scholars who have criticised third mission activity for detracting from the 'core' purpose of a university, or for prioritising commercial relationships and contract research over teaching. However, the authors find little evidence to support this, and make a strong case for embedding the third mission with research and teaching and viewing the three missions as part of the inherent make-up of the contemporary university, observing that research and teaching are now seen as (but were not always seen as) mutually reinforcing. Nabaho et al. (2022) conducted a limited analysis of the conceptualisation of the third mission in African universities and also found that it was seen as a complement to research and teaching.

Finally, this book also has relevance for higher education beyond Africa. Given trends of institutional isomorphism towards 'the research university' and the internationalisation of higher education (Zapp and Ramirez, 2019), the trajectories of large public universities in Africa help us understand the pressures and opportunities for higher education institutions globally, in particular the influence of development agendas and how local engagement can sit alongside national and international roles.

---

1   A notable exception is the work of Bekele and colleagues, who have analysed strategic plans and developed methodological frameworks to understand university-society partnerships in Africa (Bekele and Ofoyuru, 2021; Bekele, Cossa and Barat, 2021; Bekele, Ofoyuru and Woldegiorgis, 2024). The broader state of the literature is revisited in Chapter 7.

Universities in ten city regions

This book analyses local engagement at ten African flagship universities (shown in Figure 1). Table 1 provides a summary of the ten universities. The table also includes some data on the size of the universities (in terms of student numbers), their ranking in the *Times Higher Education World University Rankings 2023* (where they are included), and two rankings that examine research performance, innovation outputs and societal impact – the *SCImago Institutions Rankings* and the *Ranking Web of Universities*. There are significant issues with such league tables (Hazelkorn, 2007; Kiraka et al., 2020), and relying on rankings as a measure of 'flagship' status is deeply problematic. However, they may serve as a proxy for the prominence and international profile that these universities all seek in their strategic plans.

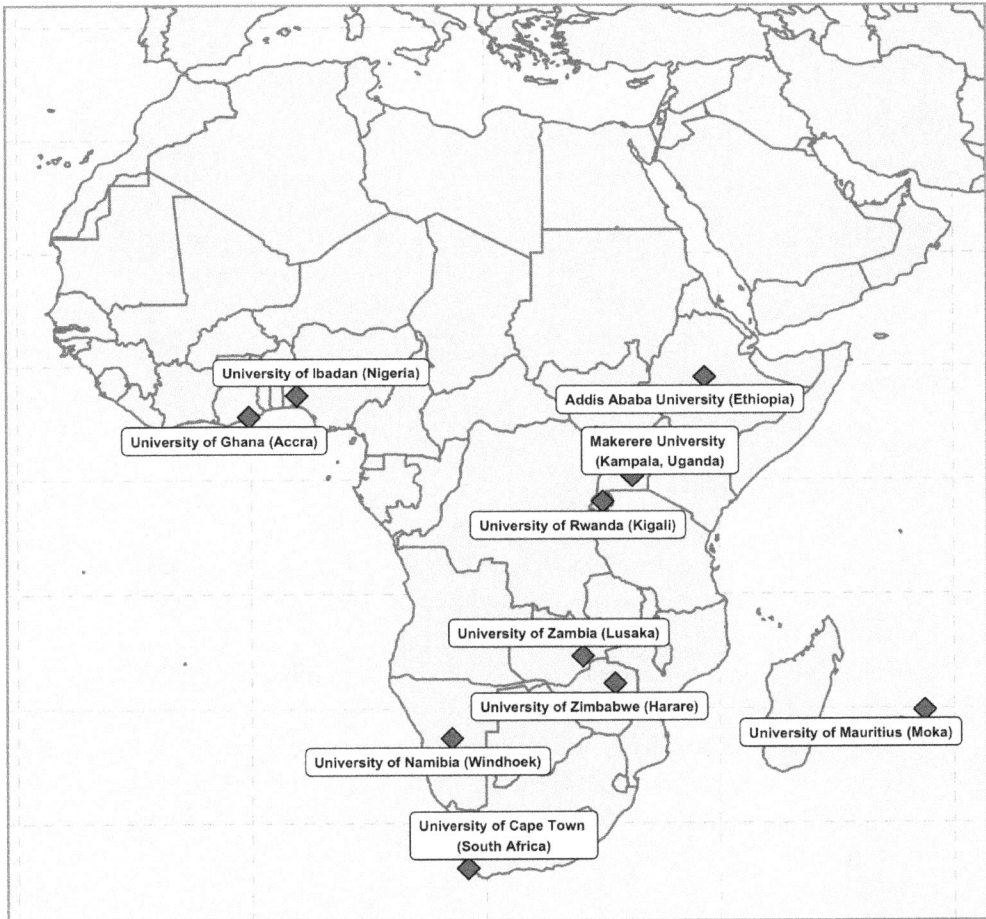

Figure 1 Map of case study flagship universities

Table 1 Profiles of case study flagship universities

Flagship university	City and country	No. of FTE students (a)	Proportion of international students (a)	THE ranking 2023 (a)	SCImago ranking 2022 (Africa (World)) (b)	Web of universities ranking (sub-Saharan Africa) (c)
Addis Ababa University	Addis Ababa, Ethiopia	46,881	0%	601-800	32 (637)	15
Makerere University	Kampala, Uganda	31,233	3%	801-1000	23 (620)	9
University of Cape Town	Cape Town, South Africa	21,069	15%	160	1 (425)	1
University of Ghana	Accra, Ghana	54,256	1%	1001-1200	34 (639)	12
University of Ibadan	Ibadan, Nigeria	26,156	0%	401-500	52 (664)	14
University of Mauritius	Port Louis, Mauritius	8,710	1%	1001-1200	116 (737)	35
University of Namibia	Windhoek, Namibia	29,369	3%	601-800	96 (716)	86
University of Rwanda	Kigali, Rwanda	28,609 (d)			89 (708)	51
University of Zambia	Lusaka, Zambia	16,903	1%	501-600	62 (677)	39
University of Zimbabwe	Harare, Zimbabwe	20,598	0%	1001-1200	74 (690)	30

(a) Times Higher Education (2023) (except where indicated)
(b) SCImago (2022)
(c) Ranking Web of Universities (2022)
(d) University of Rwanda (2018a, p. 16)

The ten flagship universities have been selected on the following five criteria, designed to provide a group of broadly comparable institutions across varied local contexts.

1. Universities can be considered a flagship university: usually a large public institution, often perceived as one of the most prestigious universities in their country, and wielding considerable influence (Chapter 2 explores the definition of a flagship in more detail).
2. Universities are located in sub-Saharan Africa, as defined by the UN (2022b). This geographic classification includes island states such as Mauritius, and excludes North Africa.
3. Universities are located in a country with English as an official national language, and English is used by the university for strategic plans and other public materials. Anglophone institutions and universities influenced by English models of education are thus well-represented, whereas Francophone and Lusophone Africa is not represented.

4. Universities are headquartered, or have the majority of their facilities and activity, in a major city region.[2] The implications of the city region as a unit of analysis are discussed below.

5. Universities had an active strategic plan in 2020, and this was either in the public domain or permission was granted to analyse and cite it.[3]

Given the diversity of higher education institutions in Africa, there are notable differences between some of the universities, despite meeting the criteria. First, they vary in size. Addis Ababa University and the University of Ghana have over 45,000 students, whereas the University of Mauritius and University of Zambia have 8,700 and 16,900 students respectively. The remainder sit within the 20,000 to 32,000 band. Second, some have a greater international profile than others. The University of Cape Town in particular is an outlier in most of the traditional metrics of research 'excellence' and global standing: league table rankings, numbers of international students, the volume of research funding, and the development of academic staff (the number of lecturers with PhDs, the proportion of postgraduate research students, and so on). Third, all ten universities have a significant presence in a major city region, but the composition of this presence varies. For example, the University of Ghana has a city centre campus in Accra, with the main Legon campus 13 kilometres north-east of this. The University of Mauritius is in Moka district, which directly adjoins the capital of Port Louis, whereas the University of Cape Town has a commanding presence overlooking the city. Yet despite these differences – and a distance between some of thousands of kilometres – there is more that binds these institutions than separates them, as we will see from the flagship profiles in Chapter 3.

All ten flagships are primarily based in a city region: an urban core with links to a semi-urban and rural hinterland (Watson, 2019, p. 3). This allows us to examine the broad local engagement activity of universities without being confined to the administrative or political boundary of a city. There are two implications worth noting. First, using city regions as a unit of analysis allows us to consider cities with different formal statuses. The University of Ibadan is the oldest degree awarding institution in Nigeria, but the university is the only one in this study not in a capital city (Ibadan is the third most populous city in Nigeria, although it was the largest in 1960 at the time of Nigerian independence). Cape Town is the legislative capital of South Africa, but the second-largest city. Nonetheless, both Cape Town and Ibadan are large cities and have the economic clout (and development challenges) to match their capital city counterparts. Second, it allows us to consider networks and linkages extending out of an urban core, and reflects the move towards a multidimensional understanding that places are more than spatially-bounded locations.

---

2   For example, the University of Malawi has colleges in the major cities of Blantyre and Lilongwe, but the headquarters and largest college are in Zomba, a much smaller city, and so was excluded.

3   This excluded several universities that would have otherwise met the criteria. For example, as of mid-2020 the University of the Gambia was recruiting for a staff member to write their plan and so was excluded. Other universities had a plan, but this was not in the public domain and the universities did not respond to requests to share it: the University of Botswana, the University of Dar es Salaam, the University of Nairobi, and the University of Sierra Leone.

The meaning of 'place' has been debated within the academic field of regional and urban studies for decades.[4] Jessop, Brenner and Jones (2008) explore the many 'turns' that have taken place in understanding sociospatial relations, and promote a fourfold approach that highlights the importance of territories, places, scales, and networks. Privileging any one dimension is, in their view, a mistake: to be place-centric, for example, treats a place as a discrete entity and ignores its broader economic, social and political linkages (Jessop, Brenner and Jones, 2008, p. 391). As a result, the coherence of 'the city' as a unit of analysis and the future of urbanisation has been challenged, with Rickards et al. (2016, p. 1539) concluding that 'materially, practically and conceptually, the figure of a neatly bounded city space has long proven illusory'. Martinez, Bunnell and Acuto (2020, p. 1101) agree that the city is no longer the default unit of analysis in urban studies, and instead 'planetary urbanisation' has prevailed: the entire world is affected by the process of urbanisation, which has no boundaries and no simple 'inside' and 'outside'. But they also acknowledge that this academic understanding takes place at the same time the city has achieved recognition and status in international policymaking. The focus of policymakers on cities has also led to universities being considered a key actor in city-based economic development strategies (Bank, Cloete and van Schalkwyk, 2018, p. 12).

However, Watson (2019, p. 6) reminds us that the notion of the city region emerged in the North, and needs to also be grounded in the South – or, more precisely, in the individual contexts of individual places. She concludes that 'one size fits all' approaches are especially insufficient when examining low-income or emerging city regions, given that assumptions made in settings in the North regarding governance structures, resources, the informal and formal economies, civil society, and historical context are unlikely to apply.

In a similar vein, Addie (2019a) has shown how universities are embroiled in the shaping of these sociospatial dimensions. Large multi-faculty institutions in particular are well-placed to transcend the physical boundaries of the city region through their activities and networks and the production of knowledge; in doing so, Addie argues, they are key actors in constructing the region. However, universities are also shaped by territorial ties such as funding and governance arrangements, and competition amongst institutions means some realign their offer to the city region, whereas others shun regional discourses and look more broadly (Addie, 2019a, p. 17). This theorisation of the dual relationship between the university and the city region – to shape and reimagine the region, but also to be shaped and be subject to it – emerged from practice in Europe and North America, and the following chapters examine the quite different context that the ten public African flagship universities operate within.

Researching African flagships

Before presenting an overview of the structure of this book, it is helpful to present a few brief methodological reflections. There is a history of debates on the possibilities of comparison

---

4   Note that 'regional' here – and in the chapters to follow – refers to sub-national areas rather than blocs of countries.

within the field of comparative education (Cowen, 2000; Green, 2003). This book seeks to illuminate the phenomenon of local engagement across flagship universities in Africa rather than provide a rigorous comparison, but the contours of comparative study are nonetheless worth briefly visiting. Teichler (1996, p. 432) states that comparative study can be indispensable for understanding a reality shaped by common international trends, but studies benefit most when they have a clearly defined hypothesis to be tested. Nóvoa and Yariv-Mashal (2003) observe that it is one of these common international trends – that of the internationalisation of education policies and the proliferation of benchmarking, ranking, and comparisons between nations – that has driven a renewed interest in comparative research. They call for comparative education studies to become less a political tool for educational policy and more a means of intellectual inquiry; a historical journey rather than a mode of governance. Two of their prescriptions in this regard are especially pertinent for this book. First, they call for the focus on comparative education to be on problems rather than facts or realities.

> *By definition, the facts (events, countries, systems, etc.) are incomparable. It is possible to highlight differences and similarities, but it is hard to go further. Only problems can constitute the basis for complex comparisons: problems that are anchored in the present, but that possess a history and anticipate different possible futures; problems that are located and relocated in places and times, through processes of transfer, circulation and appropriation; problems that can only be elucidated through the adoption of new zones of looking that are inscribed in a space delimited by frontiers of meaning, and not only by physical boundaries. (Nóvoa and Yariv-Mashal, 2003, pp. 436–437)*

Considered within their historical, political, social and economic contexts, the problems facing flagship universities as institutions, together with the development challenges facing the communities, city regions, and nations they inhabit, provides a suitable basis for such complex comparisons. Second, Nóvoa and Yariv-Mashal (2003, p. 426) note the paradox of global benchmarks and indicators serving to promote national policies in the field of education, which is perceived as a field where national sovereignty can still be exercised. In the pages that follow we can observe the complex trade-offs involved when flagship universities are subject to similar international comparisons and benchmarking (for example, competing in global university league tables, and aspiring to become a 'world-class university'), whilst also inhabiting a public, national, and sometimes local role that demands the university to adapt and be relevant to society. This complements a more sophisticated understanding of 'place' developed over the past few decades, where 'the local' has emerged from being a separate sphere where wider national or global processes are 'worked out' to an intrinsic, interconnected part of global networks and flows (Cochrane, 1998, p. 2122).

At the heart of the analysis that follows are strategic planning documents, supplemented by evidence of university collaboration, networks, and partnerships including press releases and newspaper coverage, national and sectoral development strategies, and city masterplans. These are supported by a broader review of the academic literature on African universities, local engagement, and higher education and development, published prior to 2024. These were identified by conducting a comprehensive search using multiple databases, including JSTOR, Google Scholar, Scopus, and Explore (UCL Library Services' search tool), together with backward snowballing to identify additional relevant studies from publication reference lists. Collectively, the strategies, evidence and literature were qualitatively analysed using *thematic analysis* – an iterative process of finding 'patterns of meaning' within a data set by reading, coding, and generating themes (Braun and Clarke, 2006, p. 87; 2019, p. 594).

Strategic plans are ways to balance institutional ambitions (attract international students, for example) and external expectations (such as accountability for public money) (Stensaker et al., 2019, p. 541). They can offer a window into the priorities, plans, and values of an institution, and can reflect and in turn reproduce wider societal discourses. As Tight (2012, p. 304) notes, documents such as strategic plans are not neutral or objective media but should be viewed in light of the cultural context in which they were written, and as tools to construct social reality and a version of events. Cohen, Manion and Morrison (2013, p. 34) add that policy reports in particular can reveal assumptions that underlie reforms, represent outlooks and ideologies, and embody the tensions of state policy (the limitations of strategic plans are explored in Chapter 4). The close links between flagship universities and their national governments are discussed in some detail in the coming chapters; the often complex interrelations between national governments and multilateral organisations such as the United Nations and the World Bank complicate this further.

The structure of this book

In examining the local role of African flagship universities, two separate threads of academic study need bringing together. The first, the subject of Chapter 2, is the role of African higher education institutions in development. The idea of the developmental university, the flagship university, and the role of universities in both the UN Sustainable Development Goals and the African Union's Agenda 2063 strategy are explored in turn, illustrating different framings and conceptualisations of African universities since the 1970s. The second is weaved throughout: the contribution of universities to their place and their locality, and their engagement beyond teaching and research, which has come under increased scrutiny over the past couple of decades. In a high-profile 2007 report, the OECD called for universities to 'do more than simply educate and research': they must 'engage with others in their regions, provide opportunities for lifelong learning and contribute to the development of knowledge-intensive jobs which will enable graduates to find local employment and remain in their communities'. The report acknowledged that higher education institutions have been helping to serve the needs of local economies in many countries for many years, but these links have tended to be 'sporadic rather than systematic' until recently (OECD, 2007, p. 2).

There are a few motivations that explain this shift. Driven by tightening public purse strings, there are pressures on institutions to be seen as relevant and to demonstrate societal value (Addie, 2016, p. 2), and regional development agendas (themselves also often driven by public spending concerns) usually require coordination with local partners (Chatterton and Goddard, 2000, p. 478). There are pull factors too: local engagement can bring benefits to universities, including improved community and local government relations, increased student enrolments, and income from consultancy and training. Perhaps above all, the fates of places and their universities are entwined: when one declines, all parties suffer; a dynamic recognised both in the UK and in South Africa (Christopherson, Gertler and Gray, 2014, p. 214; Bank, Cloete and van Schalkwyk, 2018, p. 2).

Chapter 3 profiles the history of the ten universities, and we see that many of the defining traits of African flagship universities today are visible in their past. With this foundation established, Chapters 4 and 5 examine the engagement activities and local development roles of all ten flagship universities through the lens of their strategic plans. Previous academic studies have used such plans as the basis for examining the role of universities in society, but predominantly of universities in North America and Europe. 'Engagement' is defined as projects, programmes, activities and relationships with external parties outside of the university. These may include research, innovation and community-focused projects, and social, cultural, environmental and economic programmes of work. Activities may be led by staff or students, or by an external partner with university support.

The traits of the modern flagship university are discussed in Chapter 6, including how flagships view their role in society and in their local area, and the factors that shape their positioning, including a framework of hurdles that need to be overcome before this local activity is expanded. Chapter 7 takes a step back to look at the significance of these topics for universities and governments, and offers suggestions for future work. To begin, we visit the 1970s and the birth of a new model of university in sub-Saharan Africa.

CHAPTER 2

UNIVERSITIES, DEVELOPMENT AND A NEGLECTED LOCAL ROLE

This chapter focuses on three key framings of African universities: the idea of the developmental university that emerged following the wave of independence in the 1960s, flagship universities – a type of university considered a 'mother' institution, often since independence and continuing to this day – and, more recently, the role of universities as part of the wider development frameworks of the UN Sustainable Development Goals (SDGs) and the African Union's Agenda 2063. The concept of the developmental university was an ideal type promoted by leaders, governments, and international organisations, calling for universities to be engines devoted to supporting national development. Flagship universities are large public institutions, often perceived as one of the most prestigious institutions in their country, and wield considerable influence. Although the ten universities in this book have been selected on the basis of being flagship institutions, several were also expected to be, and strove to become, developmental universities in the 1970s – they are not mutually exclusive.

Any work on universities in Africa taking on a development role needs to be situated in the history of African higher education institutions (HEIs) – their colonial origins, the relationship to national development projects and identities (and the influence of higher education projects from other times and places on this in turn), their proliferation and growth post independence, and their subjugation to the policies of supranational agencies in the 'lost decades' following this. This history of African higher education continues to be contested and challenged, with studies emphasising, for example, how the sheer weight of the colonial legacy continues to stymie universities today (Assié-Lumumba, 2006, p. 15; Ndlovu-Gatsheni, 2017). A failure to understand this history, and the global discourses, power relations and policies that continue to shape and constrain universities in Africa today, means any exploration of the role universities play in national – let alone local – development will be hampered.

The study of the contribution of higher education to development is not a new phenomenon. However, discussions over a successor set of global development targets to the Millennium Development Goals – which ended in 2015 – launched a fresh re-examination of the role of universities in achieving the goals, whilst revisiting older debates about the relationship between higher education and development. This chapter concludes by examining this relationship through the lens of the SDGs and Agenda 2063, and finds that the local dimension of higher education is largely missing from discussions.

A brief history of the idea of the developmental university

The idea of the developmental university emerged in the 1970s as 'an institution that in all its aspects is singularly animated and concerned, rhetorically and practically, with the "solution" of the concrete problems of societal development' (Coleman, 1986, p. 477). As McCowan (2019, p. 97) sets out, the traditional university pillars of activity take on a distinctive form: teaching focuses on courses to train professionals with the skills to meet local or national development needs, research is predominantly applied in nature and guided by national and local priorities, and community engagement takes on a greater importance – lecturers are encouraged to work as consultants and advisers to local and national government, and community outreach projects are complemented by services such as legal advice, health clinics and continuing education for adults.

Coleman's definition of a developmental university, above, views this model as an 'ideal type', a fourth variant of other concepts: Cardinal Newman's idea of the university, the idea of the modern university, and the idea of the multiversity (Coleman, 1986, p. 477). The Weberian notion of the ideal type does not necessarily correspond to pure form or actual instances, but is subjectively formed from a set of characteristics ('ideal' referring to ideas rather than a notion of perfection) (Swedberg, 2018). As such, the idea of the developmental university was far from uniform in practice. As Wandira (1981, pp. 255–256) noted, 'Mozambique, Somalia and Tanzania may, for instance, feel that universities should play an important role in the building of socialist societies. This view may, however, not be accepted in Kenya where the very definition of "African socialism" may differ from that of Tanzania … the diverse nature of African society dictates a diversity of patterns of university organisation'.

This ideal type can be traced in loose form through the outputs from three major conferences on African higher education. At the Conference on the Development of Higher Education in Africa in Tananarive (now Antananarivo) in 1962, participants agreed that African universities should be 'the main instrument of national progress' (UNESCO, 1963, p. 13). This lofty expectation continued to grow, demonstrated at a workshop of university leaders in Accra in 1973. Participants felt that the African university 'must be accountable to, and serve, the vast majority of the people who live in rural areas'. It should be 'committed to active participation in social transformation, economic modernisation, and the training and upgrading of the total human resources of the nation, not just of a small elite' (Yesufu, 1973, p. 42). In the mid-1990s, Ajayi (1996, p. 200) reflected upon the idea of the developmental university and asked the question: 'how much did all that discussion, all that protracted debate really matter? If these issues were important in determining the effectiveness of the universities' contribution to development, how can we justify the failure to resolve them? If they did not matter, then the debate itself must somehow have missed the point. What explanation can we find for this?' They conclude that the 'preoccupation with the training of manpower equipped purely with university degrees has, in major ways, put limits on the creative responsiveness of the university to other developmental problems' (Ajayi, 1996, p. 201).

Four main features characterise the developmental university model. First, it is an institution designed to serve society. Second, it looks beyond a focus on the elite and includes the poor and marginalised. Third, it aims to bring economic or social benefits to society that are non-academic in nature. Fourth, it does this by applying knowledge with practical and immediate effect – to be useful and to tackle challenges (McCowan, 2019, p. 98). As we will see, these features are remarkably similar to the principles behind the formation of land-grant colleges in the United States in the 1860s, which is unsurprising given they were used as a model for the developmental university.

Coleman detailed what an 'ideal' developmental university looks like. Sitting across the three reworked pillars of university activity are a 'formidable range of functions' which include aligning the development plans of the university with national development plans, and coordinating with public and private agencies, including across different levels of education and with other universities (Coleman, 1986, p. 485). Given many developmental universities were the sole higher education provider in their country in the decade or two following their founding, the addition of this coordinating function demonstrates how the role of the developmental university evolves over time. Coleman also presciently describes the expectations made of African flagship universities today, who often align their strategic plans with those of their government and act as mentors for education providers throughout their country – a legacy of the developmental model which persists today.

The origins of the developmental university idea

The developmental university model that took root in Africa in the 1970s was influenced by higher education movements from previous eras and other parts of the world. Coleman (1986, p. 477) traces the idea of the developmental university to three previous traditions: the land-grant universities established in each US state in the mid-nineteenth century with a focus on 'extension', Japan in the 1880s as part of a national push to a 'path of forced modernisation', and the Soviet Union, which emphasised both the 'rigorous fit' between the university and the 'manpower' requirements set out in five-year plans, and harnessing the university as a tool to fight inequalities in society and to indoctrinate students. The main ideas from both sides of the Cold War – the land-grant movement and the Soviet model – are worth exploring in more detail.

Land-grant colleges in the US arose from the Morrill Act of 1862, the 'charter of America's quietest revolution' (Taylor 1981 in Mcdowell, 2003, p. 34). The features of land-grant colleges are notable for their similarity to the idea of the developmental university, and for the break they represented with the HEIs that preceded them – a shift that would likely resonate with African leaders in the 1970s. Mcdowell (2003, p. 36) explains that the land-grant system was revolutionary for three reasons. First, its classrooms and degrees were accessible to the working classes; second, it encompassed a far wider breadth of subjects and curricula; and third, it provided access to knowledge to those who would not qualify or seek to attend traditional lessons in classrooms. As such, land-grant colleges ruptured the model of higher education – opening campuses to young people whose previous experiences was 'on farms, in machine shops, in bakeries, or in factories', and 'making the work of cow barns, kitchens, coke ovens, and forges the subject matter of their investigation'. The effect was twofold: to solve some of agriculture's practical problems, and to challenge the view that higher education was reserved for the upper classes (Mcdowell, 2003, pp. 34–35).

However, this first strand – solving problems in communities, outside of the university walls, formalised as 'extension' – only properly took off in the twentieth century. As the decolonisation of Africa took hold in the 1950s and 1960s, across the Atlantic it was the 'golden age' for land-grant universities and the extension system, with the agricultural sector 'judged as one of the most productive sectors of the US economy' (Huffman and Evenson 1993 in Mcdowell, 2003). Service and extension functions made the leap across the ocean from the early 1950s in the form of grants to universities in Africa from the United States Agency for International Development (USAID), where the land-grant model was used (Coleman, 1986, p. 780).

In the Soviet Union, the state had tight financial and political control of HEIs, which effectively become an arm of government. As Johnson (2008) explains:

> *Russian and then Soviet higher education grew from its modest domestic influence and marginal global status in the early 1900s to become one of the largest and most comprehensive systems of higher education and research in the postwar era … the close integration of higher education and science policy with the highest echelons and priorities of the Communist Party and Soviet state leadership contributed directly to these massive investments (and networks of patronage), as Soviet higher education, professional training, and research became tightly connected with the planned economy and rapid technological development. (Johnson, 2008, p. 162)*

However, this tight control led to destructive interventions into higher education and academic research by factions of the Communist Party (Johnson, 2008, p. 163). As a result, following the dissolution of the Soviet Union (and too late to provide a cautionary tale for African leaders in the 1970s), the higher education system was 'especially ill-suited to adapt to the economic crises of the 1990s' and the same factors that previously provided the backbone for higher education strength and expansion became systematic weaknesses (Johnson, 2008, p. 159). Nonetheless, Soviet higher education attracted the attention of researchers, including in the US, for the rapid, large-scale professionalisation of labour in pursuit of technological advancement (Schwarz, 1957, p. 67). This link between universities and meeting 'manpower' needs is explicit in the developmental university model, and is closely linked to the ascendency of human capital theory in the 1960s (Oketch, 2014, p. 98).[5]

---

5   This focus on 'manpower' was not confined to the public policy of post-independence African states and the Soviet Union. For example, the UK Department of Scientific and Industrial Research aimed to bring scientific research and industry closer together, and 'scientific manpower' – the provision of a pipeline of people with research skills – underpinned this (Flanagan et al., 2019, p. 15). The department was dissolved in 1965.

The land-grant and Soviet influences shared a national orientation – modernising the agricultural sector, driving a five-year plan – even if the beneficiaries may have been local: a veterinarian in Volgograd or a farmer in Fort Worth. It is worth noting that locally-focused higher education movements are not cited as antecedents: in the US, institutions such as the University of Illinois at Chicago Circle were founded as urban universities in the 1960s, with a strong focus on being locally embedded (Goodall, 1970). In England, nine civic 'redbrick' institutions, including the University of Birmingham and University of Liverpool, were founded in the nineteenth century with the stated purpose of meeting local needs (Sanderson, 2016). It is perhaps understandable that there is little evidence of African leaders or nationalist intellectuals casting their eyes to locally-oriented models of higher education. The English redbricks, for example, were funded by wealthy industrialists in major industrial cities – a difficult model to emulate in recently-independent African states (Cannadine, 2014). The local, urban focus adopted by the likes of the University of Illinois was also at odds with sweeping ambitions of national transformation; rapid urbanisation across the African continent would not become a policy concern for several decades.

Although different international models had varying degrees of influence on the developmental university – helped in part by donor money – we should be careful not to overstate the influence of any one model. Whilst the strong alignment with national needs, for example, could be considered a norm or a trend shared by other societies looking to overturn traditional models of higher education, it was also a product of the process of decolonisation and a pragmatic, necessary, single-minded focus on creating a state that could stand by itself and survive. These endogenous pressures manifested in several ways: the government needed civil servants and skilled workers, universities recognised the changing times and shifted their missions as a form of self-preservation in the face of scarce resources, and, perhaps above all, there was a 'voluntary and spontaneous sense of civic or national responsibility of university authorities and members of the professoriate, expressed individually or collectively, that the intellectual and physical resources of the university should be placed at the service of the nation' (Coleman, 1986, p. 780). These pressures are reflected in staggering growth: annual university enrolments in Africa increased nearly 11 per cent each year between 1960 and 1980 (Hinchliffe 1987 in Kamola, 2014, p. 605). The developmental university also had its own distinctive traits, some of which – such as attempts to indigenise staff and curriculum – are explored in the next chapter.

Nor should we assume homogeneity amongst the new African institutions that emerged. The 1970s saw widespread calls for newly independent governments to dismantle the 'fossilised colonial model of institution', and instead establish universities that could support the creation of inclusive societies, yet few were created in the mould of being of the people and for the people (McCowan, 2019, p. 92). Perhaps closest to this ideal was the University of Dar es Salaam in Tanzania, with President Nyerere a vocal advocate for developmental universities across the continent. Approaches diverged between institutions: Court (1980) shows how the paths of Makerere University in Uganda, the University of Nairobi in Kenya, and Dar es Salaam were shaped by their respective political regimes. Battles were also fought within institutions: campaigners at Makerere University in Uganda favoured academic freedom and traditional scholarship, whereas reformers at Dar es Salaam called for an interdisciplinary, nationalist curricula; excellence was pitted against relevance (Mamdani, 2018). These debates can be traced back to discussions amongst Western powers in the nineteenth century about the purpose of education in the colonies, and are echoed in the rich arguments between Black activists (in particular W.E.B. Du Bois and Booker T. Washington) during the civil rights movement in the US (Assié-Lumumba, 2006, p. 42). And, as we will see in later chapters, the debate continues in African societies today – with the quest for relevance appearing to dominate.

The decline of the developmental university idea

As a state-owned, state-funded institution, a high-profile developmental university had built-in limitations even before fiscal constraints and donor pressures began to hit. As Aina (2010, p. 8) notes, the 'increasingly authoritarian postcolonial political leaders of Africa in the 1970s and 1980s did not take kindly to their universities fulfilling their role of providing independent critical thinking'. Mamdani (2008) adds:

> *The University was of course an incubator of both critical thought and of a counter-elite whose critique sometimes veiled ambition. The more professors sounded like ministers-in-waiting and sometimes even Presidents-in-waiting, the more their critique began to sound self-serving. In a single party context, the university began to take on the veneer of the opposition party, giving rise to confrontations that often led to strikes and shutdowns. (Mamdani, 2008, p. 6)*

As such, 'the crisis of the developmentalist university was part of the larger crisis of nationalism' (Mamdani, 2007, p. 259). As a concept, the developmental university was used to support often controversial policies, limiting university autonomy and the scope for critical inquiry. Universities were targets of nationalist projects, and nationalist leaders had a tendency to interfere and impose their views on universities (Ndlovu-Gatsheni, 2017, p. 65; Lebeau, 2020, p. 444). There were other limitations too. McCowan (2019) summarises the critiques of Coleman and Court in the 1980s:

> *Funding and support for the universities were precarious in the context of changes in government; capacity among staff members for implementing the developmental vision was limited, given the fledgling nature of the higher education systems and institutions; many had been trained in traditional (colonial) institutions and so struggled to change their mindset; and traditional university functions of teaching and research were seen to suffer through excessive engagement of staff members with government and development agency work. (McCowan, 2019, p. 108)*

The expectations made of universities following the developmental model were significant, and illustrate the disconnect between the idea and reality. Universities were 'expected to carry the burden of African nationalism, which claimed to express African aspirations' (Ndlovu-Gatsheni, 2017). Both Coleman (1986, p. 492) and Court (1980, p. 668) make the point that effective institutions must be built before they can deliver results, with the latter noting that land-grant colleges in the US needed to prioritise their own development before that of their country – half a century passed before they became a force in national development, and the 'golden age' of land-grant colleges came almost a century after their founding. Perhaps the greatest limitation of the idea of the developmental university was the expectation of short-term results.

The oil crisis in the late 1970s and resulting recession had severe implications for the funding of African higher education. At the same time, the World Bank produced revised calculations as to the economic benefit of universities compared to primary and secondary institutions, stating that 'top priority should be given to primary education as a form of human resource investment' (Psacharopoulos, 1981, p. 333). As African governments applied to supranational institutions such as the IMF for loans, conditions were imposed that limited spending on social services, including cuts to higher education (Kamola, 2014, p. 606). Chapter 3 tells the stories of how these cuts affected several of the universities in this study; Mamdani (2018) captures the stark effects this had at Makerere, illustrating a broader phenomenon felt by many African universities:

> *By the late 1980s, the IMF had taken charge of the Ugandan treasury, and the World Bank was running Makerere's planning. The Bank proposed a threefold reform premised on the assumption that higher education is a private good. First, it argued, given that the benefit from higher education accrues to the individual, that individual should pay fees. Today, nearly 90 per cent of students at Makerere are fee-paying. Second, the university should be run by autonomous disciplinary departments and not by a centralised administration. This was achieved by means of a simple formula, requiring that 80 per cent of student fees go to his or her disciplinary department or faculty. The Bank had managed, very effectively, to starve the central administration of funds. Third, the curriculum should be revised to make it market-friendly and more professional: the geography department began to offer a BA in tourism, and the Institute of Linguistics a BA in secretarial studies. (Mamdani, 2018, p. 32)*

The repercussions are felt today: whilst Makerere attempts – in efforts reminiscent of the drive for excellence in the 1970s – to shed 'market-driven' degree programmes and cap student numbers (Kigotho, 2020), it is nonetheless keenly sensitive to graduate employability and is continuing a programme of decentralisation (see Chapter 5). Degree programmes are axed in the name of quality – but the job market is the arbiter of quality rather any intellectual or academic criteria. When it comes to relevance, however, neoliberal reforms may have ultimately served to accelerate notions introduced by the developmental university model. In their book, *Democracy and the Discourse on Relevance within the Academic Profession at Makerere University*, Felde et al. (2021)

found that recognition and status within Makerere (and other African universities) is driven by alignment with economic development and a 'knowledge economy'. Academics become consultants, short-term research is prioritised, and relevance is determined by external priorities rather than through independent academic inquiry. Perhaps we should not be surprised that the developmental ideal morphed into a more commercial model: historians have persuasively argued that the land-grant movement in the US was largely driven by economic concerns, rather than (as commonly assumed) educational ones (Key, 1996).

In summary, the rise and fall of the idea of the developmental university forms a distinct chapter in the history of the African university, preceded by the colonial model and succeeded by a market-led, managerial model. Aina (2010, p. 3) describes these periods as each introducing waves of reform to address the perceived deficiencies of the last era, and, because they are framed as emergencies, they fail to address long-term goals. The result, he concludes, is that 'the terrain of African higher education continues to resemble a thick forest of institutions, systems, and practices lacking clear and distinct tracks, values, and goals, or a mission and vision that connect the institutions and systems sufficiently to the major challenges of their contexts (whether global or local)'. Few would dispute this description. But it is one arguably shared by most, if not all, higher education systems, rather than being a distinctively African phenomenon. The developmental university idea was shaped by international models, but was nonetheless rooted in the context of African nations. The question is whether a distinctly African institution has emerged from the thick forest of institutions and the discourse on relevance.

The influence of African flagship universities

Notions of what an African university should be have evolved over time, shaped by political exigencies, societal expectations, and the pressures of international donors and lenders. Models for national development from the US or the Soviet Union gave way to the global 'massification' of higher education, hitting African universities particularly hard (Mohamedbhai, 2014). As the following chapters will show, new African universities borrowed frameworks and structures from the likes of the University of London or the University of Durham in the 1960s. By the millennium, a new university in Cameroon was running strategy workshops with the University of Manchester. Just over a decade later, planners looking to form the University of Rwanda drew inspiration from the Indian Institutes of Technology.

African flagship universities have been subject to these ideas and models, and they have been shaped by the developmental university movement and the market-led period (and the proliferation of public and private institutions) that followed. Flagships have an explicit development function, and they have needed to adapt to meet the demands of massification – not only in terms of their own student numbers, but also often fulfilling a mentoring role for other institutions in their country; just as they have often borrowed their own structures from overseas universities, in turn they create fledgling institutions in their own image. The flagship university is often the most prestigious and largest institution in the country, predominantly in the capital or at least in an urban setting, and almost always a public institution. As Teferra (2017, p. 2) notes, flagship universities wield considerable influence, 'shaping higher education systems and [standing] as flag-bearers and trendsetters of the academic ethos in their respective countries'. McCowan (2019, p. 102) adds that they are 'highly sought after by students and [have] a close relationship to government ... very often there have been struggles over the direction of these institutions, moving between more universalist, colonial and globalised orientations, or alternatively more nationalist, decolonised and locally engaged ones'. Their history as highly visible sites of national discourse and protest (see Lebeau, 2008) makes them uniquely influential yet simultaneously vulnerable to state interference.

Multi-country studies of African flagships

There are two significant academic studies of flagship universities in Africa. The first is the Higher Education Research Advocacy Network in Africa (HERANA) project funded by the Carnegie Corporation and the Ford Foundation and undertaken by the Centre for Higher Education Trust (CHET) in South Africa, with several publications providing an empirical overview of eight flagship universities in Africa over the period 2001–2015 (Bunting, Cloete and Van Schalkwyk, 2013; Cloete, 2015; Cloete, Bunting and van Schalkwyk, 2018). The second was led by Damtew Teferra and supported by the German Academic Exchange Service (DAAD) and the University of KwaZulu-Natal, South Africa, and culminated in a book edited by Teferra (2017) with contributing authors from 11 flagship universities. Table 2 indicates the six universities included in the Teferra study, and the four from HERANA, which also feature in this book.

Table 2 Involvement of case study universities in previous flagship studies

Flagship university	HERANA	Teferra
Addis Ababa University		•
Makerere University	•	•
University of Cape Town	•	
University of Ghana	•	•
University of Ibadan		•
University of Mauritius	•	•
University of Namibia		
University of Rwanda		
University of Zambia		•
University of Zimbabwe		

The HERANA study identified eight universities as the most prominent public university within their country, all of which shared broad 'flagship goals'.[6] These are: to have a high academic rating, which would make it a world-class university or at least a leading or premier university in Africa; to be a centre for academic excellence; to engage in high-quality research and scholarship; and to deliver knowledge products which will enhance both national and regional development (Bunting, Cloete and Van Schalkwyk, 2013, p. 1). The project explored the factors influencing the ability of Africa's flagship universities to 'transform themselves into research-intensive institutions' (Cloete, 2015, p. 13), whilst recognising the distinction, and tensions, between 'flagship' and 'world-class' universities (revisited in Chapter 6). In particular, the HERANA project developed the idea of a 'research-intensive flagship university', one which is 'committed to the creation and dissemination of knowledge in a range of disciplines and fields, and featuring the appropriate laboratories, libraries and other infrastructure which permit teaching and research at the highest possible level' (Cloete, 2015, p. 22). However, the authors also recognised the arguments of Douglass (2014), who maintains that flagship universities, whilst emphasising research, also have wider recognised goals and place less importance on global rankings than a university 'merely' aspiring to be world class. Nonetheless, as the HERANA project evolved and the project focus narrowed to the knowledge production function of universities, the nomenclature shifted from 'flagship universities' to 'research universities', concluding that 'only a university with certain research capacities can contribute to development' (Cloete, Bunting and van Schalkwyk, 2018, p. 23) – an assertion that would appear to depend on how 'development' is defined.

As part of the second major multi-country study, Teferra (2016) examined the 'neglected contribution' of African flagship universities, specifically enrolment patterns, profiles of academics, graduate output, and research productivity. Teferra's definition of a flagship demonstrates the breadth of their roles.

> ... *flagship universities in the African context are described as among those first higher education institutions established prior to and post-independence and have been considered as the leading institution, in their respective countries, at the present time. These 'mother' institutions would typically have the largest number of academic programs, senior academics, as well as enrolments.*

> *They are also the largest producers of graduate students, research, and publications and play an important role in national capacity building and innovation efforts. Flagship universities tend also to be the most internationalised in their countries in terms of institutional cooperation and linkages. They are also by the process of isomorphism*

---

6 The University of Botswana, the University of Cape Town, the University of Dar es Salaam, Eduardo Mondlane University, the University of Ghana, Makerere University, the University of Mauritius, and the University of Nairobi.

trend setters in their respective countries in terms of curriculum content, academic culture, and policy issues.

Flagship universities in Africa are also the most important contributors of academics to the new 'sibling' institutions. Most typically the flagship universities are based at the capitals of the respective countries and are at the heart of the social, cultural, educational, and political fabric of their nations.

Invariably flagship universities in Africa are public and urban – and are virtually all based in the nations' capitals. They are held with highest national esteem – a mother institution from where the social, political, and economic elites graduate – and maintain high clout and influence. (Teferra, 2016, p. 82)

As a framework, this definition of flagship universities captures the key characteristics of all ten universities that feature in this book: namely their size, public status and influence, and location in the capital.[7] As a set of criteria, this describes a fairly broad and diverse group of universities, rather than an 'ideal type' to which they may be aspiring towards, or are expected to become. Flagships may, however, also be under pressure to conform to ideal types, as was the case with the concept of the developmental university, and is the case with world-class universities or research universities – explored in Chapter 4.

Teferra followed up with another book in 2017, systematically examining academic staff, funding patterns, governance, leadership and management, graduation, research and publishing, internationalisation, and academic freedom within 11 flagship universities.[8] Universities were selected to ensure geographical representation including sub-Saharan Africa, 'Arab' Africa and major island states, and coverage of two major language groups – English and French (Teferra, 2017, p. x).

These two major studies of African flagship universities, whilst providing a valuable academic foundation, do not focus on the local (that is, sub-national) development role of these institutions. This book seeks to address this gap, looking specifically at engagement with communities, government, city hall and others in the local areas that flagship universities call home. It also revisits the concept of the flagship university, expanding the analysis to include three institutions not previously included in multi-country studies (the University of Rwanda, the University of Namibia, and the University of Zimbabwe), and introduces a new lens for exploring priorities, plans, and values – the university strategic plan. In doing so, this study identifies the distinctive

---

7   The most notable exception is the University of Ibadan, which is not in Nigeria's capital Abuja, or largest city, Lagos. It is, however, in a major urban area (see Chapter 1 for the full selection criteria).

8   The University of Botswana, Cairo University, Addis Ababa University, the University of Ghana, the University of Nairobi, the University of Mauritius, the University of Ibadan, Cheikh Anta Diop University, the University of Dar es Salaam, Makerere University, and the University of Zambia. 15 universities were shortlisted, but not all authors submitted work; the identity of the four omitted universities is unclear.

traits of modern flagship universities, and their role in the development of sub-Saharan African city regions.

The tension between consultancy and service

As the profiles of the ten flagships will show, traits that appear distinctive in the modern flagship model often have historic roots; the university is both a reflection of how society changes and a key actor in its evolution. African flagships today carry an inheritance from the developmental university and the decades that followed, and this is illustrated by the tensions between consultancy and service that continue to this day.

The idea of the developmental university was conceived in part to make a contribution to development through 'service activity'. This meant academics serving on committees, conducting evaluations, helping to inform national policy, and sometimes undertaking private consultancy work – all of which were seen as helping to address priority problems, but also distracting staff from teaching responsibilities (Court, 1980, p. 662). Coleman (1986, p. 492) agreed that the benefits of academics working on 'real life problems' was substantial, from increased productivity and public recognition to allowing the university to retain top staff. However, the attention of researchers shifted to meeting the needs of external bodies, it resulted in overcommitment and a diffusion of interests ('frequently resulting in superficiality'), and teaching and university service suffered. The result was 'commercialised scholarship', and Coleman cited consultancies paying $300 per day (over $800 today) – a substantial sum for a public sector employee in a low-income country. Writing about the experience of academics in Nigeria, Yesufu (1973) explained that university salaries were so uncompetitive that staff were forced to either work elsewhere, or supplement their income through private salary. This was not well received.

> *Civil servants openly frown on what is generally referred to as 'outside commitment' of university staff. This allegation of outside commitment has been so trumpeted as to portray university staff as money-mongering vampires, who neglect their university teaching and research, and concentrate instead on private businesses. It has gone to the ridiculous extent that student examination failures have come increasingly to be blamed on 'absentee professors and lecturers' engaged in private business. Every time a lecturer is not located in his office, it is presumed he is on 'outside commitment'. Of course, the truth is that some university staff do have outside commitments and even private businesses. But it is equally true that those of them motivated primarily by private greed are in the minority, and much of their commitment is generally in [the] academic and public interest. (Yesufu, 1973, p. 265)*

These tensions survived the developmental university era. In 1996 three former African vice chancellors reflected on the future of universities in a report for the Association of African Universities, and lamented the trend of university staff running businesses alongside their core academic roles. In a commentary in *African Affairs*, a reviewer noted that the three vice chancellors ignore the 'problem of feeding and educating one's children, often on less than £1,000 per year' (Peil, 1997, p. 124). As many universities have become more commercially-minded and budgets for staff remain limited, these pressures persist today with the 'consultancy culture among some academics in low-income countries being a significant distraction from teaching and research responsibilities' (McCowan, 2019, p. 108). Mamdani (in Kamola, 2014, p. 606) argues that the 'galloping consultancy culture' and 'the NGO-isation of the university' is the result of a decades-long push towards a market-driven model of African higher education. However, marketisation may have merely served to validate and institutionalise consultancy work: the low salaries and tradition of balancing multiple roles that encouraged 'outside commitment' in the 1970s both survived the developmental university era and are powerful motivators for staff to seek additional income.

McCowan (2019, p. 98) distinguishes between the developmental university focus on serving society and the entrepreneurial university focus on generating income through consultancy – which is sometimes also badged as serving society. The developmental university primarily serves the state and knowledge is produced with this in mind, whereas the entrepreneurial university – which emerged in the 1990s – 'follows whichever paymaster happens to be present'. We can also learn once more from land-grant colleges. Mcdowell (2003, p. 43) argues that both consultancy activities and public service can make positive contributions to scholarship, and indeed for many academics consultancy is their main source of exposure to real-life problems. However, he adds that 'usefulness' needs to be judged in terms of societal benefit: 'the notion has long been rejected that what is good for General Motors is good for America'.

The line between pure service work for local or national development and commercial consultancy will inevitably blur, especially with the near-universal pressure on universities to generate and diversify income. These tensions are evident in the analysis of strategic plans that follows. The priorities and mandates of multilateral agencies or philanthropic organisations can further muddy the waters, a point we return to in Chapter 6. Dependence on external funding sources (leading to little discrimination in which work is accepted, a dilution of mission and focus, and encroachment into teaching and academic research), or reliance on state funding without a degree of independence or the ability to be critical, are both problematic. This book argues that the modern flagship university is neither a spiritual successor to the developmental university, nor a corruption of its ideals, but rather a pragmatic organisation carefully and continuously balancing a complex set of pressures.

However, old concepts have a tendency to resurface – reformed and reworked to meet new challenges and changing contexts. Mtawa (2019, p. 60) tracks the 'revitalisation' of the developmental university model over the past decade or so, in particular calls for universities to strengthen their societal mission. For McCowan (2019, p. 92), the advent of the Sustainable Development Goals has given the idea of the developmental university 'a new lease of life'. We now turn to the role of universities in continental and global development agendas.

Higher education and development goals

Agenda 2063 is a 50-year continental strategy offering 'a robust framework for addressing past injustices and the realisation of the 21st Century as the African Century' (African Union Commission, 2015, p. 1). Seven aspirations are translated into 20 goals and 174 targets. An 'education and skills revolution' will be driven by high-quality technical and vocational education centres, strong links between education and industry, investment in universities, science and innovation, increased academic mobility across the continent, and harnessing 'universities and their networks ... to enable high quality university education' (African Union Commission, 2015, pp. 14–15). African universities will play an important role in achieving all seven aspirations, even if higher education is not explicitly mentioned within these.

The strategy was broadly welcomed by higher education observers, albeit with one eye firmly fixed on the scale of the challenge (Ufomba, 2020). Universities need to align programmes with Agenda 2063 goals, work closer with industry, revise curricula to both meet labour market needs and embed Pan-African ideals, form new creative partnerships, and expand access (Mutisya, 2018; Kajela, 2022). African governments need to integrate Agenda 2063 into their national education plans, policies and curricula from basic to tertiary levels (Addaney, 2018). Given the vital role of higher education in achieving the goals, universities require sustained investment to enhance access and quality, develop research infrastructure, and effectively expand virtual learning – strategic government funding and partnerships with the private sector are key (Okebukola, 2015; Leresche, 2021). But the scale of the agenda, and the long-term framework in particular, also opens up new opportunities for universities beyond their contribution to the goals – for example, an increased demand by policymakers for systematic policy research, a need universities are ideally positioned to meet (Mutisya, 2018, p. 9). The need for policymaking capacity is underscored by the presence of multiple goal frameworks for governments and universities to navigate – including the most globally prominent of them all, the Sustainable Development Goals (SDGs).[9]

At the global level, the 17 SDGs were adopted in September 2015 by all 193 UN members. Goal four ('ensure inclusive and equitable quality education and promote lifelong learning opportunities for all') includes explicit reference to higher education: 'ensure equal access for all women and men to affordable and quality technical, vocational and tertiary education, including university', and 'substantially expand globally the number of scholarships available to developing countries ... for enrolment in higher education' (UN, 2015, p. 19). Yet, as we will see, the other goals will also require the participation of HEIs to be successful.

The SDGs build on the eight Millennium Development Goals (MDGs) adopted in 2000. The world has changed substantially since then, and this is somewhat reflected in the goals – not least the emphasis on global sustainability and reducing inequality. Significant changes

---

9   Agenda 2063 and the SDGs are 'highly aligned and strongly linked', and share an institutional framework designed to integrate with national plans (Kithome, 2019). These are not the only strategies replete with goals and indicators that policymakers need to pay attention to – see, for example, the 10-Year Strategy of the African Development Bank Group (2024-2033), which is 'built on' Agenda 2063 and the SDGs (AfDB, 2024, p. 5).

have also taken place since 2015, and the impact of the COVID-19 pandemic means 'an urgent rescue effort for the SDGs' is needed (UN, 2022a, p. 2). As we enter the final half-decade before the 2030 end date, progress is slipping on many of the targets, including those for higher education (UN, 2023).

The United Nations Development Group led the process of formulating the SDGs, and tried to address the widespread criticism that the MDGs were too top-down (for example Bond, 2006). A process of 100 national consultations formed a 'global conversation' on the content of a set of post-2015 goals, including capturing the voices of 22,000 people on the role of education in the goals. However, this conversation was perceived as being dominated by experts and agencies in the Global North (Soudien, 2013, p. 839; Chankseliani, Qoraboyev and Gimranova, 2021, p. 112). Power imbalances have also played out in wider education debates, with the World Bank seen as being able to shape education policy through the use of funding mechanisms in low- and middle-income countries to a greater extent than UNESCO; the former tending to favour a human capital approach to education that focuses on the skills needed to increase productivity and growth, and the latter emphasising rights-based and capability-driven approaches that give individuals the freedom to do what they value (Regmi, 2015, p. 564).

How are the SDGs relevant for African flagship universities? As a global development compact, national governments are the primary signatories to the goals, and flagship universities – given their size and prominence – have an outsized role in national development; any government taking the goals seriously will depend on the contribution of its largest universities. As Chankseliani and McCowan (2021, p. 6) observe, many universities have been doing the kinds of development-oriented teaching, research and engagement activity demanded by the goals long before the SDGs were formulated, and this is especially true for flagship universities. Nonetheless, a few flagship universities have stated ambitions to align their activities around SDG priority areas (Chapter 5), reflecting both the influence of global agendas and a close relationship to national development.[10] The content of the goals, the assumptions and trade-offs inherent in their formulation, and how these are translated at national level, are therefore likely to have an outsized impact on a flagship university compared to, for example, a small private institution, and as such are important to examine.

Direct and indirect contributions to the SDGs

The SDGs call for both greater access to and greater quality of all levels of education. Ilie and Rose (2016, p. 435) note that wide inequalities in access are present in primary and secondary education in many countries, and that as levels of higher education participation increase, so do wealth and gender inequalities within higher education. They conclude that unless inequalities

---

10 As such, the greater environmental emphasis in the SDGs has repercussions for flagships, which will be expected to lead their higher education sectors in terms of changes to the curricula, campus sustainability and other climate change policies. Given their size, they may have a large impact through the number of students they educate (McCowan, 2020, p. 14).

earlier in the system are addressed, we are highly unlikely to reach the higher education access target set in the SDGs. Reconciling quality with wider (and more equitable) access brings significant challenges, in particular in countries with limited resources. Attempts to address this through, for example, the dual track approach of government and private funded places within the same institution (as seen in East Africa) risks a deterioration in quality, increased teaching loads, and the erosion of time for research (Oketch, 2016, p. 532).

Issues of quality and access relate specifically to goal four, on education itself. It is here where the higher education sector plays a direct role. Yet universities have an indirect role in many of the other goals, even if they are not explicitly mentioned. Ensuring healthy lives and promoting wellbeing (goal three) requires trained health professionals. Sustainable industrialisation may call on the expertise of universities, and encouraging innovation and increasing the number of research and development workers will require active and engaged universities (goal nine). Indeed, professional, scientific and technological knowledge and training are required to deliver all of the goals (Unterhalter, Peppin Vaughan and Smail, 2013, p. 819).

In addition to contributing directly and indirectly to the goals themselves, higher education has a wider, cross-cutting role; Unterhalter and Howell (2021, p. 13) describe these as 'instrumental' and 'intrinsic' pathways respectively. The intrinsic pathway includes convening networks and partnerships, and providing a space for debate and critical review. Through these activities, universities can help develop social cohesion, especially in societies recovering from conflict (Smith, 2013, p. 807). HEIs may also have a role in the collection and analysis of data and the contextualisation of results (Unterhalter, Peppin Vaughan and Smail, 2013, p. 819).

Higher education is in an unenviable position in relation to the SDGs. Universities will play a wide role in tackling each of the goals, but will largely be judged on access to higher education – an easy-to-measure target but one that is in part dependent on addressing wider inequality – and quality – a difficult-to-measure target requiring education systems to reconcile widening access and uniform quality within financial constraints. This is complicated by the interdependence of the different stages of the education system – the quality and equity of primary and secondary education determines access to (and completion rates for) higher education; the quality of teacher training is dependent upon the universities or training colleges that provide it. Ilie and Rose (2016, p. 452) stress the need for a 'system-wide approach' that recognises this interplay between different stages of education.

Furthermore, concerns over Northern dominance of the goals has been reflected in fears of Western universities 'promoting a standardised model of education and the hegemony of Western knowledge', driven in part by their commercial interests (Barrett, 2013, p. 826). Whilst there is much that universities could usefully learn from different higher education models, there is little acknowledgement of the variety of higher education traditions around the world, how vulnerable they may be to the decisions of supranational agencies, and to the understanding these agencies have of what makes for a 'good' higher education sector (McCowan, 2016, p. 507).

Barrett (2013, p. 826) described the SDGs as 'the most significant re-balancing of the notion of international development since the concept of international development emerged in the

1950s', but bemoaned the lack of articulation of this within the education debate. Others have said that education as a whole was not prioritised by the high-level panel overseeing the discussions over the goals, and called for a louder voice from the higher education community (Sayed and Sprague, 2013, p. 790). However, Unterhalter, Peppin Vaughan and Smail (2013, p. 820) recalled the 'perverse consequences' of the MDGs and argued against a specific target for higher education, and instead encouraged discussion on the role of secondary and higher education in addressing poverty, sustainability and equality. Given the role that education can play in reproducing inequalities (Unterhalter and Howell, 2021, p. 9), a strong case can be made for a university that plays a more equal role in development, focused on reducing inequality, meeting the needs of society, and inculcating these values in students (Boni and Walker, 2016). Furthermore, whilst the goals may have a limited (although ambitious) explicit role for higher education in widening access and delivering quality, there is a far wider role for universities in delivering the other goals, which will draw upon the boost to social development and economic growth that higher education can bring, but require deliberate work to do so in an inclusive and equitable way.

Academic discussion on higher education and the SDGs has focused on issues of access and quality, the direct and indirect role of universities in the goals, and on the wider framing of higher education as a means to human capital formation. From an institutional perspective, the focus has been on individual implementation of the SDGs – from campus sustainability to curricula reform (Serafini et al., 2022). There has been little discussion of the broader spatial role of universities within these debates, and little recognition of the relationship between universities and local places and communities – as education providers, development actors, and centres for innovation and skills training in towns, cities and rural areas. A similar pattern emerges around Agenda 2063 discussions, although Mutisya (2018, p. 19) notes that collaboration between universities and industry provides a platform for creating and implementing the ideas, knowledge and innovations that Africa needs for inclusive growth, green development and resilience at the local level, and Addaney (2018, p. 188) argues that integrating Agenda 2063 into university curricula will enable graduates to positively shape their environment and society.

The missing local dimension

A decade and a half ago, the OECD (2007, p. 17) proclaimed that the region can be seen as 'a laboratory for research projects, a provider of work experience for students and a source of financial resources to enhance the global competitiveness of the institution'. This portrayal of the region as a source of bountiful opportunity for the university rather than an equal partner has perhaps been more nuanced in practice, although financial diversification doubtless remains a factor in regional engagement. Tuunainen (in Nelles and Vorley, 2010, p. 6) details the evolution of the third mission, growing from 'commercialisation and licensing to encompass a wider range of activities ranging from the application and exploitation of knowledge in an economic domain to harnessing the social and community orientated capabilities of universities'. Trippl, Smith and Sinozic (2012) show how third mission activities in several countries are converging towards broader societal objectives. More recent contributions have called for third mission activity to be strengthened (in this case in South Africa) by building the capacity of communities as well as that of the university (Petersen, Kruss and van Rheede, 2022). Bank, Cloete and van Schalkwyk (2018, p. 9) explain how third mission activity over the past two decades sought to engage more effectively with local communities, and has morphed into 'a new vision of universities as place-makers'. Compagnucci and Spigarelli (2020, p. 20) warn of isomorphism – the tendency to emulate 'world-class' universities – in third mission activity. But frameworks such as global and continental development goals also shape activity.

The shortcomings of using goals to inform development policy have been well articulated by scholars (for example, Fukuda-Parr, 2017). Global development goals are a political tool – a measurable set of targets and indicators that allow straightforward comparison and policy formulation. Although goals may engender accountability and political commitment, they prioritise clarity over complexity, single issues rather than interconnectedness, the tracking of trends in a 15-year vacuum rather than a longer-term historical framework (Agenda 2063 has positive longevity in this respect), and – crucially – nations and continents rather than sub-national areas.

It is therefore unsurprising that discussion on the role of universities in the SDGs and Agenda 2063 is predominantly national-focused, and exists quite separately from the literature on the local role of universities.[11] The broader literature on the SDGs does, however, have a local dimension. Lucci et al. (2016) have asked whether cities are on track to achieve the SDGs by 2030. Jiménez-Aceituno et al. (2020) have looked at local bottom-up initiatives in Africa; Mejía-Dugand, Croese and Reddy (2020) looked at SDG implementation in cities in the Global South in the context of the pandemic. Moreira da Silva and Kamal-Chaoui (2019) estimate that at least 100 of the 169 SDG targets can only be achieved globally through the involvement of sub-national governments.

As such, the local role of universities and their relationship with sub-national governments is pertinent to broader discussions on higher education and the SDGs and Agenda 2063. A better question than 'how relevant are the SDGs for African flagship universities?' may, therefore, be 'what local role should flagships play in helping to meet the SDGs?' Flagships have a presence in many major African cities and towns, are designed to educate and train the workforce of tomorrow, and often provide an important economic and social and urban regeneration role. In some cases, the university provides an array of other services – medical treatment, electricity, internet access, venues for community events and corporate meetings (McCowan, 2016, p. 511). SDG goal 11 calls for inclusive and resilient cities – universities can play an important role in meeting this goal through their dual role as being physically 'of' the

---

11 There is some discussion of the need for regional partnerships between countries to help governments learn from each other and build higher education capacity – for example Owens (2017, p. 418). Chankseliani, Qoraboyev and Gimranova (2021, p. 116) attempted to view higher education contributions to the SDGs through a 'glonacal' (global, national, and local) lens in Kazakhstan and Georgia, but merged the local and national categories when the challenges identified for each were broadly similar; they do, however, acknowledge that HEIs may need to work with local government to support local communities (2021, p. 120).

city, but also by shaping its future development; urbanisation itself crosses several of the goals: healthcare, education, and climate change.

This chapter has introduced African flagship universities, institutions that, in some cases, were closely linked to developmental states and aspired to the developmental university model, and were later shaped by global trends in the structure and delivery of higher education, including massification. Although land-grant and Soviet university models may have influenced the idea of the developmental university, there was a contemporary of the new wave of African institutions that perhaps better illustrates what many large, African universities later became. In early 1960s California, Clark Kerr introduced a new model of public research university, and another ideal type: the 'multiversity'.

> *The multiversity is not only larger but has many more "moving parts". The multiversity acquires ever more "accretions", the product of new opportunities and new problems, yet when conditions change it cannot rid itself of those accretions. In the multiversity there is an irreducible plurality of communities, functions, disciplines, internal interests, external constituencies, agendas, and beliefs. (Marginson, 2016, p. 23)*

The 'accretions' of the US multiversity include administrative functions and external consultancy. For African flagship universities, accretions arrived upon the tide of marketisation and massification: increases in student numbers, new disciplines and courses, engagement with policymakers and businesses, regional campuses, and a mentoring role for other HEIs. Those universities following the developmental university model often reverted to being traditional flagship institutions (McCowan, 2019, p. 97), later bringing further accretions as new frontiers opened: from consultancy and skills training to international partnerships and SDG targets. As the national focus widened to accommodate international obligations, has there also been a local turn? Do flagships play a role in their communities? If so, have the responsibilities of universities to the towns and cities they call home become a further accretion? This book seeks to answer these questions. First, however, we need to get to know the ten universities: their origins, their roles, and the challenges they face.

CHAPTER 3

THE EVOLUTION OF TEN FLAGSHIP UNIVERSITIES

Many of the defining traits of African flagship universities today are visible in their past: complex relations with government, the circulation of staff between higher education and civil service, a mentorship role for the national university sector, the impact of alumni, a quest for relevance. As Tikly (2019, p. 41) has demonstrated, colonial legacies strongly influence education policies and structures today; we ignore the force of path dependency in setting the trajectory of institutions and systems at our peril. Understanding the history and evolution of flagships therefore helps us to understand some of the roots of the tensions they face today between their developmental origins and the expectations of society, a tension that defines the nature of their local engagement activity. Although previous studies shed light on the battle between two polarised perceptions of the flagship university – a great national institution driving growth and development, or a beleaguered, near-bankrupt monolith outmanoeuvred by newer, more nimble competitors – none in doing so illuminate the role of flagships in their local areas. The reality for most flagships sits somewhere between these two poles, a position that has evolved and continues to shift, opening up new local and international engagements alongside their historic national role.

This chapter profiles the ten flagship universities in turn. First, the historical origins and contexts are described, covering the establishment and evolution of each university. The middle sections cover institutional governance and how the university contributes to the nation – for example, through policy influence and workforce development – as well as the relationship with government. The final section covers challenges, summarising the issues and limitations faced by the university. The universities are ordered from the oldest – the University of Cape Town – to the newest, the University of Rwanda, formed in 2013.[12]

University of Cape Town (Cape Town, South Africa)

Few institutions better embody the role of universities as sites of national debate and contestation than the University of Cape Town (UCT). Founded in 1829 as the South African College, a high school for boys, UCT became a full university in 1918. British colonialist Cecil John Rhodes and

---

12 Based on the date the institution was awarded independent university status. Many had predecessor colleges of higher education that long pre-date their current structure.

his business associates provided substantial funding and, later, land for the university, in part with the aim of healing Boer-British animosity in the Union of South Africa (Crowe, 2017; UCT, 2020a). Historian Howard Phillips stresses the importance of understanding the roots of the South African higher education system when policymakers undertake reforms (which they frequently do: South Africa's Higher Education Act was amended nine times between 1998 and 2013 (Cloete, Bunting and van Schalkwyk, 2018, p. 187)). A simplistic analysis might trace these roots back to the British model, given the colonial heritage. But, as Philips points out, there was no single British model of higher education, with South Africa's first two teaching universities – UCT and Stellenbosch – 'enthusiastically embracing' the Scottish university system (explained by the preponderance of professors and senior administrators from Scottish universities at the South African College). Scotland's major universities in the nineteenth century were characterised by the provision of both a liberal education and professional training, and marked by an emphasis on hard work and frugality rather than aristocratic heritage – a contrast to Oxford and Cambridge (Anderson, 1995, p. 23). The features of this model, from the structure of degrees to the teaching methods, were then replicated by the subsequent waves of universities set up in South Africa over the next 70 years (Phillips, 2004, p. 122).

The UCT website describes the university's reputation as 'Moscow on the Hill' for its opposition to apartheid in the long decades before the 1994 elections (UCT, 2020a). Phillips, who has written a history of UCT, sees the relationship between UCT and the apartheid government as more mixed, and that 'until UCT has recognised both its beauty spots and its warts and confronted them directly, it will not easily be able to go into the future unequivocally' (UCT, 2020b). He describes two other important shifts in this period. The first is the change from a teaching institute to one focused on both research and teaching, which led to today's framing of the university as research-led. The second is 'the beginnings of indigenisation of teaching and research', with the first seeds of UCT considering itself an African rather than European university (UCT, 2020b). This recognition continued to grow in subsequent decades, and manifested itself in the recent explosive calls for decolonisation of South African higher education.

UCT was a key site of nationwide student protests which erupted in 2015-16. These were driven by two factors: the #RhodesMustFall movement protesting the culture of historically elite, white universities such as UCT, and the #FeesMustFall movement against the exclusionary cost of higher education. The protests, though rooted in legitimate opposition to a discriminatory higher education system, nonetheless 'traumatised' staff and students, and threatened the notion of universities as spaces for free expression and debate (Jansen and Walters, 2019, pp. 23–24). The roots of these protests also lie in a system – and in particular elite institutions within the system – unprepared for the vast increase in students and expectations of change, creating a 'political pressure cooker' (Bank, Cloete and van Schalkwyk, 2018, p. 15).

The student protests were notable for their violence at an institution no stranger to fierce debates. Ntsebeza (2020) gives an overview of the dramatic twists and turns of the field of African studies at UCT, a subject deeply intertwined with the university's understanding of itself and its role in South African society – and Africa more broadly. The School of African Studies in its various guises (from Bantu Philology, to informing a 'Native policy' in the lead-up to apartheid, to its temporary abolition in favour of interdisciplinary research in the 1970s) is partly the story of power struggles in UCT leadership. Ntsebeza (2020, p. 13) contrasted the vision of former UCT vice chancellor Max Price for the university to be an 'Afropolitan university' against a lack of support for the school, and called for the current leadership to take African studies more seriously if it truly wishes for UCT to take on a leadership role amongst African universities, as is reflected in UCT's strategic plan. The debate over African studies at UCT serves as a reminder of how individual academic fields within an institution can reinforce or undermine the broader strategic mission of the university.

UCT is something of an outlier in this book given the comparatively greater resources and international prominence of the university. However, given the tensions between fulfilling this international role (with the pervasive discourses and policy pressures that accompany it), and the significant needs of South African society, the difficulty of reconciling the past with the development needs of the present, and the esteem with which UCT is held as a research-led flagship university across the continent, means its inclusion is valuable.

Within South Africa UCT is a medium-sized institution, but it is especially strong for research output: the university was home to three per cent of public university students in 2015 (a relatively high proportion of these are at postgraduate level), but produced 17 percent of research articles over the period 2010 to 2016 (Cloete, Bunting and van Schalkwyk, 2018, pp. 192, 203). Maintaining academic standards whilst opening access has – in common with other South African universities – created tensions, but also necessitated a close focus on core functions. Bank, Cloete and van Schalkwyk (2018, p. 15) suggest that this has been at the expense of adopting a more outward-looking orientation. UCT is also subject to challenges facing the South African higher education sector more generally: from insufficient public funding to meet growing enrolments (Ashwin and Case, 2018, p. 6), to a perceived failure of the state to drive a place-based public good role for universities in the country (Molebatsi, 2022, p. 177).

Addis Ababa University (Addis Ababa, Ethiopia)

Addis Ababa University (AAU) was established in 1950 as the University College of Addis Ababa, before becoming Emperor Haile Selassie I University in 1961, and taking its current name following the overthrow of the Emperor in 1975 – a process in which the university was a key site of resistance that led to the new military government (Teferra, 2017, p. 13). Enrolment was low in the early years – 4,500 in a country with a population of 34 million – and the staff were all expatriates (in particular from the USA and UK), a practice that shaped the educational philosophy and introduced English as the language of instruction (Ayalew, 2017, p. 108).

In contrast to many flagship universities in other African countries, AAU was – at least in theory – unencumbered by colonial education structures. Whilst the university escaped the constraints of a single higher education system imported from a European metropole, external influences nonetheless dominated, with American aid playing a particularly outsized role (Gilbert, 1967, p. 6). Planners saw an opportunity to create an 'Ethiopian institution under Ethiopian leadership', and the result was an eclectic system with challenges of integration: AAU's leaders needed to reconcile a Swedish-influenced technical school and German engineering college into a single Faculty of Technology, and a British medical school with a US programme for training district health officers, for example (Wodajo, 1973, p. 244). The opportunity to realise an indigenous, bottom-up conceptualisation of a university does not appear to have been successful. The challenges of integrating different departmental and faculty models was complicated by the dependence on foreign staff; in the words of Balsvik (2005, in Ayalew, 2017, p. 138), 'one may wonder what was worse: an Ethiopian teacher unqualified to teach the foreign curriculum, or a foreigner unqualified to see the curriculum in the proper Ethiopian perspective; and both necessarily adopting a defensive attitude to the content of the educational material'.

Today Ethiopian universities are subsidised by the government, with students contributing through a deferred payment taxation mechanism for graduates (Ayalew, 2017, p. 125). The relation between AAU and the state has historically been an uneasy one (as has been the case with other flagship universities), with Human Rights Watch reporting widespread government interference in AAU affairs and the suppression of academic freedom in a 2002 report; several senior AAU administrators and at least five professors resigned in protest (Human Rights Watch, 2003). AAU has numerous other challenges which it also shares with other flagship universities: shortages of qualified staff, inadequate IT and laboratory resources, and rigid financial and human resource policies (Ayalew, 2017, pp. 122–123).

Despite widespread challenges, the university plays an important role in national development efforts. This role has roots in the historical mission of the university as a service-oriented institution and not an ivory tower, and working to meet 'manpower' requirements in the early decades by creating special courses for statisticians and sanitary workers, health workers and geologists (Wodajo, 1973, p. 246). Under the Ethiopian University Service, all students spent an academic year working 'in the provinces', getting to know their country and their people (Wodajo, 1973, p. 248).[13] In recent years, and as the higher education system in Ethiopia greatly expanded, AAU supported new regional public universities and private higher education institutions through the training of staff, shaping of curricula, direct teaching and supervision, and the provision of models for governance and organisational structure. AAU is, as Ayalew puts it, the 'mother institution' for Ethiopian higher education (2017, pp. 140–141). This indirect influence, felt across the country, is important for considering the local and national impact of flagship universities.

AAU has also long provided research and consultancy to Ethiopia's public and private sectors, given the concentration of qualified staff at the university. Ayalew highlights national projects

---

13 This programme was apparently opposed by most students at its inception, and was seen as a form of payment for government-funded education (Gilbert, 1967, p. 8). Given the strong influence of the US land-grant university model on the formation of AAU (Gilbert, 1967, p. 6), and on developmental universities more generally, one could speculate whether such a model was at least partially inspired by the US Peace Corps programme (founded 1961), and the concept of 'service'. The Ethiopian University Service programme was discontinued (Tamrat, 2019), but programmes of national service for graduates exist in Ghana (NSS, 2020) and Nigeria (NYSC, 2020); both programmes were established in 1973 and have an explicit focus on national development efforts.

including railways, road construction projects, and the construction of the Renaissance Dam that have benefited from AAU expertise – but most of this was not centrally managed by the university, and staff tend to 'moonlight' as consultants alongside their day jobs as lecturers (2017, p. 143). As explored in Chapter 2, a culture of juggling multiple jobs may help to build the experience and contacts of academic staff, but often has a negative effect on teaching and research at the university. An Office of Community Service was established at AAU in 2011 to coordinate the provision of training and consultancy services to government departments, business and other organisations, but 'striking success stories in this regard have not been easy to witness' (Ayalew, 2017, p. 143).

This concentration of expertise naturally lends AAU to being the hub for research activity in Ethiopia, with links forged with institutions across the world. These research efforts have, however, been criticised as fragmented and not aligned to national development priorities (Ayalew, 2017, p. 132). Significant research support, in particular to build infrastructure and related 'capacity building' activity, has come from donors such as the Swedish International Development Agency (SIDA), who have been active at AAU since 1980 (Ayalew, 2017, p. 126). Recent efforts to focus research efforts through specific institutes at the university, who in turn drop their teaching programmes, have been met with protest from staff, who wish to see a greater alignment between teaching and research (Nega, 2018); a focus on interdisciplinary thematic research as a means of tackling societal problems has been more warmly received, despite challenges in implementation (Wirtu, 2020).

University of Ghana (Accra, Ghana)

The University of Ghana was established as the University College of the Gold Coast in 1948 in association with the University of London, and renamed in its current guise in 1961 when it became a full university. The education system in Ghana was modelled on the British system, with the aim of training future civil service staff. During the 1960s a University of Ghana graduate (then few in number) was regarded by some as instantly employable in the public service, 'for his mind was so trained that he could turn his hand to almost anything' (Dickson, 1973, p. 104).

The role of the University of Ghana shifted over time from a Cardinal Newman-inspired view of a university (his work was reputed to be a favourite textbook in the 1960s), to an institution focused on Ghana's practical development concerns. Dr Kwame Nkrumah, the first president of Ghana and the first chancellor of the university, sardonically asked how the study of the Classics could help with the building of the Volta Dam; scholarships were introduced for students studying science subjects. By the 1970s the university offered diplomas in areas requested by government ministries (Dickson, 1973, p. 107).[14]

---

14 Dickson (1973, p. 107) contrasts the University of Ghana to Fourah Bay college in Sierra Leone, where students took the same exams as students at the University of Durham, thus requiring no knowledge of Sierra Leone or West Africa. As such, the University of Ghana was seen as 'shedding its colonial skin' quicker than some other regional counterparts. Yet Nkrumah's concern over the utility of degrees persists in Ghana today, with even the university's vice chancellor bemoaning an excess of humanities graduates and 'educated joblessness' (Aryeetey and Baah-Boateng, 2016, p. 20).

The university has been a site of national debate and contestation, with a sometimes uneasy relationship with both military and civilian governments. Nkrumah attempted to use the university as a platform for promoting his socialist ideology and continent-wide policies, with his supporters organising a 'reign of terror' against students and staff. Jerry Rawlings came to power in a 1979 coup and was initially accepted by students, but relations deteriorated as Rawlings came to view radical students as an obstacle to his ambitions (Acquah and Budu, 2017, p. 174).

Before 1992 the president of Ghana was the chancellor of all public universities; following the 1992 constitution, universities have notionally had more independence. The chairman of the Governing Council of the University of Ghana is appointed by government, but the chancellor and vice chancellor are appointed by the University Council (Acquah and Budu, 2017, p. 162). All education institutions fall under the responsibility of the Ministry of Education. The government remains a major funder of the University of Ghana, contributing 55 per cent of the budget – but down from 90 per cent a decade earlier. The university considers reliance on this subsidy to be 'a liability' (University of Ghana, 2014, p. 5).

The HERANA project examining Africa's flagship universities concluded that the University of Ghana is 'predominantly an undergraduate teaching university', with the numbers of postgraduate students (viewed by the project as a proxy for research intensity) failing to keep pace with a rapid increase in undergraduates (Cloete, Bunting and van Schalkwyk, 2018, p. 120). HERANA researchers also found that engagement projects 'are not connected directly to community needs, nor are they producing new knowledge characteristic of a research-led university' (Cloete, Bunting and van Schalkwyk, 2018, p. 119). Acquah and Budu (2017, p. 205) add that the University of Ghana is poorly integrated in national development strategies, as links between economic and higher education planning are weak. The university itself has been honest about its challenges in its strategic plan, acknowledging issues around bureaucracy, overcrowding and inadequate teaching (University of Ghana, 2014).

Despite these shortcomings, University of Ghana academics regularly serve on public boards and committees, and as experts for bodies such as the National Economic Council and National Development Planning Commission. Commentary on the government budget from the Institute of Statistical Social and Economic Research (ISSER) at the university is 'looked up to' every year (Acquah and Budu, 2017, pp. 196–197).

Finally, the University of Ghana has extensive geographic reach. The university has three campuses, and operates satellite campuses in each of Ghana's ten regional capitals. It also supports smaller, newer institutes and colleges, supporting their academic course and administrative capacity. Such a role is seen as a 'national duty' but takes up significant resources and is rewarded with little compensation (Acquah and Budu, 2017, p. 174). This institutional mentoring is a little-recognised hallmark of the modern flagship university.

University of Ibadan (Ibadan, Nigeria)

The University of Ibadan was established in 1962. Previously University College Ibadan, a degree-awarding external college of the University of London set up in 1948, and in turn emerging from the Yaba Higher College, established in 1932 to support the colonial administration, the University of Ibadan is regarded by some commentators as 'Nigeria's premier university' (Udegbe and Ekhaguere, 2017, p. 295). However, and unlike in smaller countries such as Namibia or Mauritius, Nigeria is also home to other large public universities that played important roles in decolonisation and development from the 1960s onwards (Livsey, 2017, p. 2). The University of Nigeria at Nsukka, for example, was founded in 1955 as an independent university modelled on the US land-grant universities, and could also lay claim to being a flagship university (Ndlovu-Gatsheni, 2017, p. 65).

The fortunes of the University of Ibadan have been closely intertwined with those of the Nigerian state. Materu, Obanya and Righetti (2011) explore the shifting prospects of the university over several waves of change: the University of London years (1945-62), the era of the nascent national university (1962-66), and the 'turbulent' years (1966-99). The second, and briefest, phase highlights three themes commonly with other new flagships. First, criticism from some politicians over the courses offered, their relevance to Nigeria's developmental needs, and a desire to shift to a more indigenous model of higher education. Second, Ibadan played the role of mentor to the next wave of new Nigerian universities in places such as Ile-Ife and Zaria. Their vice chancellors were trained at Ibadan, and links and influence ran deep. Third, new international relationships were established. In the case of Ibadan, this meant programmes and facilities funded by the Ford, Rockefeller, and Nuffield foundations (Materu, Obanya and Righetti, 2011, pp. 229–232). One such funder, the MacArthur Foundation, has become in recent years a significant donor to the university, with capacity-building grants shaping institutional decision-making, including moves towards being a mainly postgraduate university (Udegbe and Ekhaguere, 2017, p. 297).

There are 265 universities in Nigeria (116 are state or federal universities; the remainder are private), with the sector experiencing tremendous growth over the past few decades (National Universities Commission, 2024). Activity is regulated by the National Universities Commission, which has restrained the autonomy of institutions by, for example, enforcing governance, leadership, and management structures and restricting new programmes of study (Udegbe and Ekhaguere, 2017, pp. 299, 307). Such restrictions are not new. Periods of military rule from the 1970s onwards led to tensions over academic freedom and institutional autonomy; this period is also marked by the proliferation of new institutions, with the government keen to ensure an even distribution of universities throughout Nigeria's regions. This had three major implications for Ibadan (Materu, Obanya and Righetti, 2011, pp. 233–234). First, experienced staff left for better-paid positions at the new universities. Second, government funding was stretched across more institutions, so revenues fell at Ibadan. And third, greater competition led to Ibadan pushing into new areas to attract students and spending exceeded the available budget. The crises endured by the university throughout these 'turbulent years' have led to a legacy of dated infrastructure, brain drain, and limited funding (Udegbe and Ekhaguere, 2017, p. 312). Crises continued through bouts of military rule in the 1990s, with the international student population dropping from 2.5 per cent in the 1980s to 0.5 per cent, and staff fleeing abroad (Udegbe and Ekhaguere, 2017, p. 332).

Challenges around staff retention remain particularly problematic today. As with other flagship universities, Ibadan is – as a prestigious national university – a magnet for scholars. In turn, it is also a fertile recruitment ground for other institutions and for the government. As of 2017, there were around 30 Ibadan professors serving as vice chancellors at other Nigerian universities, or as senior government officials (Udegbe and Ekhaguere, 2017, p. 315). The esteem with which Ibadan staff are held does, of course, bring benefit to the university, which has been able to contribute to national policy formation and other developmental efforts. National collaborations can have a ripple effect as approved policies serve as a blueprint for policymaking at state and local government levels (Udegbe and Ekhaguere, 2017, p. 335).

Meaningful community engagement has proven more challenging. According to Onwuemele (2018, p. 33), policies at the University of Ibadan to encourage community engagement have few incentives (such as being linked to promotion criteria), are not aligned to other institutional policies on research or intellectual property, and do not provide guidance on how much time should be spent on community engagement (and in any case, some staff understood community engagement to mean interacting with the university community). As one senior member of university management explained:

> Teaching, research and community service are the core mission statement of the university. In terms of balancing the three activities, within the university there is no law on specification of time allocated in the three; but I know that in some universities, they say 25% to teaching, 70% to research and 5% to community service. I must confess, there is nothing like that here. The primary responsibility is teaching. But there is argument that teaching should be part of promotion criteria. This is because teaching is the fundamental thing … (University of Ibadan manager in Onwuemele, 2018, p. 34)

Formal policies are important signals. They dictate what is valued in terms of working towards promotion, and prioritisation in the face of large workloads and limited resources. Vague or high-level policies will therefore limit community engagement activity, and any engagement that occurs may instead be to serve a separate agenda – such as research to be published in an international journal – rather than to work with and to benefit the community itself.

Despite these concerns, Ibadan has worked closely with a few communities to develop community-based research and service over many decades. These 'field laboratories' include a community health programme in the village of Ibarapa, coordinated by the government, donor agencies, and the university and resulting in over 160 research articles published in international and local journals between 1963 and 1988 (Udegbe and Ekhaguere, 2017, p. 324) – the programme continues today (Chapter 5).

University of Zimbabwe (Harare, Zimbabwe)

The University of Zimbabwe was established as the University College of Rhodesia and Nyasaland in 1952 in Harare (then Salisbury), the capital of a federation covering present-day Malawi, Zambia and Zimbabwe, with degrees issued by the University of London.[15] When the federation was dissolved in 1963, the institution continued as the University of Rhodesia until independence in 1980, when it became the University of Zimbabwe. The expansion of the higher education sector was first mooted by the University of Zimbabwe itself in 1982 in a report on the inability of the university to meet the manpower requirements of the country, suggesting a new campus or institution be established (Shizha and Kariwo, 2012, p. 10). A wide consultation that followed led to the formation of the National University of Science and Technology as the second public university in Bulawayo in 1991. As higher education enrolment expanded in the 1990s against the backdrop of a collapsing economy, further universities were formed. These were geographically distributed to try to ensure all regions had a university, and were often developed as extensions to the University of Zimbabwe, cloning structures and regulations and then adapting these to meet provincial needs (Kariwo, 2013, p. 228; Gaidzanwa, 2020, p. 91).

The rapid expansion of the sector had several consequences for the University of Zimbabwe. First, the shift to a market-based model of higher education forced institutions to become entrepreneurial, described by Gaidzanwa (2020, p. 94) as the 'McDonaldisation' of Zimbabwe's universities: delivering 'fast' education on a huge scale all year round. Whilst income may have increased, at least on paper, classrooms and student accommodation became overcrowded, facilities and services suffered, and overworked teachers dropped their research and community engagement activity. Second, low job satisfaction coupled with the broader economic and political climate led skilled university staff to flee the country (Shumba and Mawere, 2012), with Zimbabwe becoming perhaps the best known and best studied example of brain drain in the 2000s. Despite these challenges, the University of Zimbabwe remains the country's most popular destination for students, and the leading producer of scientific knowledge (Lemarchand and Susan, 2014, p. 70). Academics have also been able to engage with industry, although the extent of this is unclear; a UNESCO report provides an example of the Department of Mechanical Engineering at the university conducting over 30 production assessments of Zimbabwean companies (Lemarchand and Susan, 2014, p. 36).

It is the political sphere rather than the economic one, however, that has most significantly shaped the University of Zimbabwe. Cheater (1991, p. 195) notes that there is a 'long and

---

15 Southern Rhodesia (now Zimbabwe) was regarded as the economic heart of the federation, benefitting at the expense of Northern Rhodesia (now Zambia) which produced of many of the primary exports such as copper. Urban development (and the white population) was concentrated in Salisbury (Chigudu and Chavunduka, 2020, p. 2). This had clear ramifications for the University of Zambia, formed to meet the needs of the newly independent nation in a way which Zambia's leaders felt the University College could (and did) not do.

honourable history of protest against state politics' at the university, although relations between students and government began to markedly deteriorate in 1987 when Prime Minister Robert Mugabe became executive state president, and – as per the 1982 University of Zimbabwe Act – became chancellor of the university. The subsequent history of protests, violence and the complete erosion of institutional and academic autonomy is told in detail by Cheater, and her account is in itself an act of considerable bravery given her status as an academic staff member at the time. She concludes (bearing in mind that her account is written ten years after independence) that the destruction of the university, and the silencing of staff and student 'dissidents' is viewed by politicians of new, weak states as necessary to consolidate their position, but that 'tomorrow, their persecutors will probably face the same fate' (Cheater, 1991, p. 206).

However, state control of the university intensified over the next three decades. Later accounts, such as that of Gukurume (2019) covering the tail end of the Mugabe regime in 2016 and 2017, describe a campus overrun with state security agents, where surveillance, imprisonment and brutality against students is commonplace, and academic staff are forced to self-censure. The campus became a political battleground: the ZANU-PF government saw the university community as supporting the opposition MDC party, and as such viewed controlling the university as essential for holding power (Gukurume, 2019, pp. 765–766). Although African flagship universities have often been sites of national debate and contestation (including several others in this book), the University of Zimbabwe stands out for the degree of complicity of some senior university staff.

> *The former university Vice Chancellor Professor Levi Nyagura was largely viewed by my interlocutors as Mugabe's 'blue-eyed boy', directly appointed by the President. My participants told me that Nyagura acted as an authoritarian 'hatchet man' who cracked down on opposition political sympathisers on campus. For instance, I was told that academics aligned to MDC had little chance of being promoted. (Gukurume, 2019, p. 766)*

This elision of the boundaries between the university administration and the ruling political party helped foment generations of student and academic activists that have shaped, and continue to inform, Zimbabwe's politics; one former activist described the University of Zimbabwe as 'a conveyor belt into national politics' (Hodgkinson, 2013, p. 883). Student protests, arrests, and allegations of human rights abuses have continued throughout the pandemic; Human Rights Watch accuses the government of using COVID-19 public health measures to control the opposition, including students (Gora, 2021).

University of Zambia (Lusaka, Zambia)

Unlike many flagship universities formed in Africa in the wave of decolonisation and independence in the 1960s, the University of Zambia had no direct predecessor. Zambia (then Northern Rhodesia) was notionally covered by the University College of Rhodesia and Nyasaland in

Southern Rhodesia (now Zimbabwe) before independence, an institution affiliated with the University of London. The University of Zambia opened in 1966 as a fully-fledged degree awarding institution, two years after the country's independence. The university was established to respond to the needs of the country, with – again unusually for flagships in former colonies – no relationship with any British universities (University of Zambia, 2016). Despite the desire for autonomy and a clean start, the university was still shaped by external influences. The very commission that advocated a break from the British model and set the agenda for the University of Zambia was led by Sir John Lockwood, former vice chancellor of the University of London. The initial funding for the university was provided by the British and Japanese governments (Phiri in Kragelund and Hampwaye, 2015, pp. 86–87). And as late as 1974, 87 per cent of academic staff were expatriates (Masaiti and Mwale, 2017, p. 485).

Today, the university has much in common with other flagships. Investment in infrastructure and facilities have not kept pace with great increases in enrolment (the University of Zambia is home to just over half of students in public universities), research output is low given poor funding relative to the size of the institution, and the prestige and strong reputation of the university sits alongside reports of graduates 'roaming in the streets' looking for employment (Masaiti and Mwale, 2017, p. 494). Whilst a far greater proportion of current academic staff are Zambian than in the 1970s, a shortage of qualified staff and 'brain drain' continue to challenge the university. Pipelines of trained staff and centres of academic expertise take generations to develop, and interruptions to these pipelines have long-term consequences. A 1996 Ministry of Education report paints a stark picture of the impact of staff leaving for overseas posts:

> *The loss that Zambia has suffered through this exodus is serious. Between 1984 and 1994 the University of Zambia alone lost over 230 of its lecturers, 161 of them being PhD holders with considerable degree of seniority. This is 60% of its current total number of staff. The loss to the country, in terms of investment in training and expertise, is immense. The loss to the institution, in terms of replacement needs, disrupted programs, and demoralisation of ongoing staff, is incalculable. (Ministry of Education, Zambia in Masaiti and Mwale, 2017, p. 497)*

However, concerns of qualified staff shortages and pipelines are perhaps misplaced given the state of the University of Zambia's finances today. The university is 'technically insolvent', has been unable to pay pensions or utility bills, and is cutting staff numbers by 40 per cent, resulting in pleas to the government to increase financial support (Mumba, 2021, p. 24).

The University of Zambia nicely illustrates two further traits of flagship universities. The first is their role as institutional mentors, significantly contributing to the development of national higher education systems. The University of Zambia has a history of affiliating with new institutions in the country before they become independent, creating new universities, transferring staff to manage new institutions, and of senior staff retiring from the university and establishing private universities. Masaiti and Mwale (2017, p. 510) make the point that transferring the University of Zambia model – either directly through the adoption of regulations and structures, or indirectly through the practices and cultural norms of the staff involved – offers reliability and sustainability, but perhaps at the expense of innovation and efficiency. As of 2017, the University of Zambia provided mentorship to more than 30 colleges and universities, and external examination for more than 20 colleges (Masaiti and Mwale, 2017, pp. 510–511).

Second, relationships between flagship universities and the government are often complex. Although University of Zambia lecturers can (and do) speak out against government policies, the dependence on government funding and allegations of government influence in university decision-making processes (Mupeta et al., 2020, pp. 679–680, and discussed in Chapter 5) raise questions over the autonomy of the institution. Yet the university also exerts influence within government: nearly two thirds of senior government officials and members of parliament are University of Zambia graduates, academics often serve in government as ministers or officials, university departments provide research and consultancy services to government departments, and university academics wrote the previous government's manifesto (Masaiti and Mwale, 2017, pp. 512–513).

The focus on public good and national need embedded at the foundation of the university persists in government policy frameworks and, at least in part, in the form of *civic innovation* and *civic entrepreneurship* – described in a study of how such work is embedded in university governance by Mupeta et al. (2020, p. 676) as 'the free contribution of time and effort to a project for the greater good of society without expectation of financial benefit'. The authors found that government, students, lecturers, and the public actively support the implementation of civic innovation, but barriers include bureaucracy, financial constraints, the decentralised structure of schools and departments, and the hierarchical nature of the university, in which junior voices are not always heard. Where initiatives such as healthcare provision to local communities takes place, there are twin drivers: to improve the quality of care, and to reduce the costs of delivery (Mumba, 2021).

The limited funding for societally-focused activity partly explains the drive towards internationalisation within Zambian higher education, and at the University of Zambia in particular – where the perceived economic benefits of participating in 'global markets' have led to a surge of activity (Masaiti and Mwale, 2020, p. 9). This includes the establishment of a Confucius Institute at the university in 2010, building on a history of cooperation between China and Zambia. Although framed as a shift from the power imbalances of traditional 'partnerships' led by countries in the Global North towards equitable South-South cooperation, Kragelund and Hampwaye (2015) conclude that exerting soft power is instead the underlying driver.[16] As such, the pattern of external influence in Zambian higher education that began during the formation of the University of Zambia continues today.

---

[16] This conclusion is echoed in other studies of Confucius Institutes as instruments of Chinese foreign policy and soft power; see, for example, Lahtinen (2015).

University of Mauritius (Port Louis, Mauritius)

The University of Mauritius was founded as a developmental university at independence in 1968, with three schools focusing on agriculture, industrial technology, and administration. The university has since grown in subjects and students, and the Faculty of Law and Management now produces the largest number of graduates and the Faculty of Agriculture the fewest (Li Kam Wah, 2017, p. 271). The shift from agriculture to law and management reflects global higher education trends, but also the importance of the service sector to the Mauritian economy – services form a higher proportion of the economy than in any of the other nine countries studied (World Bank, 2019b). The higher education sector in Mauritius has also grown to 65 institutions, of which ten are public and four are degree-awarding (Li Kam Wah, 2017, p. 257).

Given Mauritius is a small island state, and the University of Mauritius is the major higher education provider and research institution located within the only major city region in the country (Port Louis and adjacent towns), the distinction between the university's 'local' and 'national' engagement efforts is less prominent and less meaningful than in the other African flagship universities profiled. Three examples illustrate the tight proximity of university and state in Mauritius.

First, Mauritius aims to become a world example of sustainable development and the university has supported the government in designing a development roadmap (Li Kam Wah, 2017, p. 281). The university has also aligned its mission with the UN Sustainable Development Goals, in particular SDG 9 (to build resilient infrastructure, promote sustainable industrialisation and foster innovation). According to a former vice chancellor, 'in all our endeavours, we strive to keep the SDGs at the centre of our focus' (Jhurry, 2020). Curricula are designed to reflect national efforts to promote sustainable development, faculties (such as science, technology and agriculture) have been merged to encourage the translation of research and teaching into local impact and bring together cross-cutting SDG issues (climate change and food security, for example), and the university is part of a consortium of eight small island state universities looking at green energy. A quarterly newsletter aims to inform the public of the university's SDG work.

Second, the HERANA project found the University of Mauritius to be unique amongst the eight flagship universities studied in that university leaders and government shared the same perspective of the role of the university in national development (Cloete, Bunting and van Schalkwyk, 2018, p. 34). In other HERANA countries, national government had a strong view of universities as 'engines of development', but these were rarely translated from science and technology policies and grand national vision statements to university strategies. The authors found a strong 'pact' between government and university in Mauritius, with both adopting the 'engines of development' discourse. Such a pact, they conclude, is 'essential' for institutions to contribute effectively to development (Cloete, Bunting and van Schalkwyk, 2018, p. 31).

Third, political and governance tensions have tested academic freedom. This is not, of course, unique to smaller states, but does stand out in a nation ranked top in Africa for political governance and control of corruption (the Ibrahim Index of African Governance cited in

Jonker and Robinson, 2018). A 2012 audit report found there was 'a general view among University staff that the council [the governing body of the university] must be allowed to work more independently, in order to preserve the autonomy of the university … council must reinforce its position to manage any perception of interference in its internal affairs as this poses a reputational risk to the University of Mauritius as an autonomous institution' (Tertiary Education Commission of Mauritius in Li Kam Wah, 2017, p. 284).[17] A manifestation of this alleged government interference, exacerbated by internal disagreements, was a rapid turnover of vice chancellors from 2010 onwards, described by Li Kam Wah as the university's 'leadership problem' (2017, p. 294).

In addition, academic staff are prohibited from participating in politics (for example, standing in elections), but ostensibly enjoy academic freedom. Ramtohul (2012), an academic at the university, argues that this freedom is ultimately constrained by the university's reliance on government funding (the university is unique amongst Mauritian institutions as most students do not pay tuition fees). As such, academic freedom 'operates under a subtle veil of threat', with most academics reluctant to criticise government policy; over time the popular understanding of 'academic freedom' has morphed from free expression into flexible working hours (Ramtohul, 2012, pp. 16–17). One consequence of this is the relatively strong influence of the private sector, and weak influence of academics, in national policy formation processes (Ramtohul, 2012, p. 16; Jonker and Robinson, 2018, p. 239).

In common with other African flagship universities, the University of Mauritius has struggled with academic staffing levels, postgraduate recruitment, and research output – all hallmarks of a 'research led' university – in part due to government emphasis on increasing tertiary enrolment through undergraduate recruitment (Cloete, Bunting and van Schalkwyk, 2018, p. 273). World Bank funding in the 1990s helped procure equipment, but specialist machinery is only replaced or upgraded when consultancy or other one-off projects allow. The impact of limited funding and resources is exacerbated when university employees serve on government boards or commissions.[18] However, high staff mobility combined with a large pool of influential alumni (including ministers, a president, and academic leaders at the University of Mauritius and other institutions) have served to reinforce the university's role in national development through providing a qualified workforce (Li Kam Wah, 2017, pp. 265–266). And, although concerns are raised here too about the employability of graduates, the university has oriented its programmes towards the service industry, reflecting government economic planning and Mauritius' strategic geographic position as a 'gateway' between Africa and Asia (Cloete, Bunting and van Schalkwyk, 2018, p. 116; Jonker and Robinson, 2018).

---

17 The University of Zambia strategic plan expresses a near-identical sentiment (see chapter 5).

18 Li Kam Wah (2017, p. 282) lists some examples: a Commission of Enquiry on Education, the Commission of Enquiry on the Bus Industry, the Committee on Legal Education, the Fact-Finding Committee on Land Use of Public Lands, the Truth and Justice Commission.

Makerere University (Kampala, Uganda)

Makerere College was established in 1922 as the first higher education institution in East Africa, and to serve the British colonial administrations in the region. The college later formed part of the University of East Africa, before becoming an independent national university in 1970. The early 1990s marked the third distinct era for Makerere: that of a university influenced by neoliberalism, following periods as a colonial and then a national institution (Bisaso, 2017, p. 426). Institutional autonomy was granted to Ugandan universities in the early 2000s.

Neoliberal reforms led to a push to recruit privately-sponsored students, a focus on decentralisation of faculties (one aim was to enable entrepreneurial leaders to respond to the market), and pressure to prioritise interdisciplinary research at the expense of deepening discipline-based expertise. According to Mamdani (2007, p. x), a prominent Ugandan academic, the result of this drive towards commercialisation was the erosion of institutional integrity and educational quality, and an institutional crisis. When the World Bank began to reappraise the view of higher education as simply providing a private good in a free market, Uganda's Museveni government 'held on to the dogma with the tenacity of an ideologue' (Mamdani, 2007, p. vii). The neoliberal model has widened access and allowed far greater numbers to study at Makerere, but the quality of education has been widely critiqued (Bisaso, 2017, p. 440).

The university has established the Makerere University Private Sector Forum (MUPSF) to work with other actors for national development, and has institutionalised other mechanisms for engaging in national policymaking, including a process in the mid-2000s to focus on human resource development for decentralised local government districts by developing new curricula in medicine, agriculture, computer science, engineering, and physical planning (Musisi in Bisaso, 2017, p. 468). The university is setting up grant offices in each of the ten colleges to coordinate community engagement activities, under the auspices of the centralised Directorate of Research and Graduate Training. This is part of a shift from *outreach* to *knowledge transfer* (framed as a shift to mutually beneficial partnerships from paternalistic relationships; see Chapter 5), but, according to an analysis by Cloete, Bunting and van Schalkwyk (2018, pp. 117–118), this function remains 'ad hoc and poorly managed' and disconnected from wider knowledge production efforts. This is partly explained by promotion criteria – Kaweesi, Bisaso and Ezati (2019, p. 1) find that although academics are producing knowledge useful for policymakers and society, the emphasis is on publishing scientific research in reputable journals – but also, as will be seen, by the nature of funding.

Makerere shares many traits of other African flagship universities: beginning as an exclusive provider of higher education and now a central part of a far larger and more competitive market (a proliferation of private institutions, and regionally-distributed public universities); a history of educating many of Uganda's political elite; a critical mass of researchers and research programmes far outweighing that of other institutions and taking on a leadership and capacity-building role as a result; and significant resource and capacity challenges. However, a particular trait emerges in recent discussions over Makerere, one shared by other flagships but pronounced in Uganda: the role of donors in research.

Makerere has received significant funding from international donors, mainly for research. This funding is around three million USD a year, or six per cent of the university budget, and is seen as critical for supporting long-term research programmes at the university given the limited government funding for research (Ssembatya, 2020, p. 11).[19] Kaweesi, Bisaso and Ezati (2019) found that, perhaps unsurprisingly, academic research is increasingly driven by donor interests, and as a result the research agenda is drawn from a global perspective and not necessarily that of the university. The authors note that although legal frameworks governing research partnerships mean that any funded research will be aligned to national priorities, the lack of a secure funding base for community-oriented research means this strand is often neglected at Makerere.

University of Namibia (Windhoek, Namibia)

After the University of Rwanda, the University of Namibia (UNAM) is the youngest of the flagship universities surveyed in this book. In common with many of its continental counterparts, the university has roots in an older institution, in this case the Academy for Tertiary Education, formed in 1980 as the first higher education institute in colonial Namibia. The binary model of South African higher education – elite research universities and black teaching institutes – was extended to Namibia, with the Academy placed firmly in the latter category with a focus on liberal arts, education and public administration (Kirby-Harris, 2003, p. 360). UNAM was formed in 1992, two years after independence. The relatively recent formation of UNAM sheds light on the challenges of establishing a flagship university.

The founding vice chancellor and his team 'enthusiastically' built the university almost from scratch, improving access and achieving gender representation within ten years (Amukugo, 2017, p. 86). Gone was the apartheid higher education model, replaced by the curricula, traditions and structures of the British system (Kirby-Harris, 2003, p. 360). Despite the 'powerful symbolism' of this new university ushering in a post-colonial era (White, 1998, p. 134), a nation-building focus on education, service and development, and a rapid expansion in student numbers, geographical representation proved challenging. The majority of UNAM's facilities and programmes were concentrated in the central capital city of Windhoek, despite large swathes of the population living in the north of the country. Outreach remained a core goal of the administration, but the desire to develop a 'coherent personality' trumped decentralisation and engagement outside Windhoek was largely through distance education via the Centre for External Studies (White, 1998, pp. 134, 150). Over time, however, 12 campuses have opened across the country to improve geographic participation (Amukugo, 2017, p. 86). A UNESCO policy review (2016, p. 77) suggests developing these campuses to follow the model of the University of Rwanda – developing

---

19 Comparable figures for other flagships are hard to find. However, research income accounted for at least 23 per cent of total university income at the University of Cape Town in 2020, roughly 94 million USD (UCT, 2021a).

specialised colleges with some autonomy, but able to collectively respond to current national and global needs – and to consider decentralising even further as per the University of Nairobi, the University of Dar es Salaam or Makerere University. In time, the authors suggest, these specialised colleges could be transformed into full universities (UNESCO, 2016, pp. 77–78).

There are several implications. First, any decentralisation would need to be balanced by effective linkages. Coordination between UNAM and the Polytechnic of Namibia (now the Namibia University of Science and Technology) proved an issue following independence and led to the formation of the National Council for Higher Education in 2003 to better coordinate the higher education on offer (Amukugo, 2017, p. 87); UNESCO (2016, p. 73) themselves concede that gaps remain between higher education and vocational training. Second, Namibia has a population of around 2.5 million – five times smaller than Rwanda in an area 31 times larger (World Bank, 2019a). Specialised institutions need to be sustained by a critical mass of students and well-trained staff; although enrolment has grown, Namibia lacks qualified staff (UNESCO, 2016, pp. 71–72). Third, the experience of UNAM suggests the need for new universities to establish themselves, to centralise, before they can consider decentralisation. This institutional maturity likely takes decades, and decentralisation (despite a popular policy prescription) should be approached with caution: the mixed success of market-driven decentralisation at Makerere (Chapter 5) and the transformation of small public institutions into colleges under a university umbrella in Rwanda, a centralising effort, suggests the need for highly-personalised approaches based on individual contexts.

Although UNAM was founded 30-odd years after, for example, the universities of Ghana and Ibadan, it shared many of the same tensions in its childhood and adolescence. Friction arose between the government's view of the university as an instrumentalist tool for national development, and the university's view of itself – borrowed, as elsewhere, from the British model – as an independent bastion of academic inquiry (Kirby-Harris, 2003, p. 360). Limited autonomy meant UNAM could develop existing courses, but had less freedom to initiate new ones (White, 1998, p. 159). Yet institutional leaders were often drawn from the same pool as, and mixed with, government officials. This meant a high degree of formal and informal consultation of university staff on government policy, a complex relationship which meant UNAM had strong influence but also responded to 'unarticulated' government policy – for example by establishing programmes in areas aligned to government interests, and distance education – to try to increase the university's bargaining position with the state (Kirby-Harris, 2003, pp. 366–368). That new nation states were struggling through the same growing pains as their flagship universities perhaps explains the close yet tense relationships between the two.

UNAM continues to share issues in common with its flagship peers. The employability of graduates and relevance of the curricula is questioned (UNESCO, 2016, p. 75), despite schemes established to provide students with work experience, on-the-job training and 'practical' skills (Shaketange, Kanyimba and Brown, 2017). Research and outreach work is determined by the availability of external funding and is therefore ad hoc, with no specific strategy for research at the university (UNESCO, 2016, p. 76). However, a priority of the Multidisciplinary Research

Centre at UNAM is to collect and study indigenous knowledge, viewed as an important means of understanding the livelihoods and ensuring the resilience of local cultures (Chinsembu and Hamunyela, 2015, p. 362).

University of Rwanda (Kigali, Rwanda)

The University of Rwanda has two origin stories. The first begins with Rwandan independence from Belgium in 1962, and the request of Grégoire Kayibanda, first president of Rwanda, for international assistance to set up a university. As Gendron (2007, pp. 64–65) explains in his account of the outsized role of the Canadian government in this process, the new leadership was keen on maintaining links with the French language and Christian faith, but ideally without the colonial baggage of France or Belgium. This paved the way for Father Georges-Henri Levesque, a Canadian priest and professor of social philosophy, to be appointed the first rector of the new National University of Rwanda (NUR) in 1963. The NUR became one of the largest Canadian aid projects during the 1960s, and millions of dollars of support continued until the mid-1990s (Gendron, 2007, p. 85).

The NUR was based in Butare (now officially Huye), leading the city to become the academic and intellectual heart of the country and attracting students and researchers. Over time, the presence of the university helped to form an academic corridor between Butare and the capital Kigali, joining long-standing medical and administrative corridors (Jaganyi et al., 2018, p. 65). The NUR was implicated in the 1994 genocide, and the role that academics played is a subject of annual reflection at the University of Rwanda today. 'While the National University of Rwanda's motto was to be the light and service to the people, the university never walked the talk to prevent the genocide', said former vice chancellor Professor Alexandre Lyambabaje in 2021. 'The role of the [NUR] in the preparation and execution of the 1994 genocide against the Tutsi was significant', added a historian based at the university (Mbonyinshuti, 2021b).

The second story tells the origin of the University of Rwanda half a century later. Whereas a key driver for the NUR was to stem the flow of students studying abroad and not returning (in particular to neighbouring DR Congo), a major impetus for the formation of the University of Rwanda was consolidation. Existing public degree-awarding institutions were seen as too small and inefficient; although concerns were raised by staff that some of these were still young and needed time to grow, the Minister of Education stressed that the new institution would retain the specialisms of its predecessors, rather than becoming a set of geographically-distributed colleges offering the same curricula (The New Times, 2012). In an echo of the role of the international community in the formation of the NUR, an international review was conducted, and support was provided by the Association of Commonwealth Universities, SIDA (Sweden's government agency for development cooperation), and American foundations (MacGregor, 2014). The University of Rwanda was formed in 2013, merging seven institutions: the National University of Rwanda, the Kigali Institute of Science and Technology; the Kigali Institute of Education; the Higher Institute of Agriculture and Animal Husbandry, the School of Finance and Banking, the

Umutara Polytechnic Higher Institute, and the Kigali Health Institute. James McWha from Northern Ireland, a former leader of universities in Australia and New Zealand, became the first vice chancellor. His top three priorities for the new institution were access, research, and community engagement (MacGregor, 2014).

Today there are six independent, self-governing colleges at the University of Rwanda, spread across nine campuses, including three in Kigali. The majority of the Board of Governors, including the chair (a Canadian), are appointed by Presidential Order, although the university has the autonomy to appoint the chancellor (this role was previously given to the Minister of Education). The university sits within the wider higher education apparatus of Rwanda: there are 40 higher education institutions, 60 per cent of which are in Kigali; all but three institutions are private, enrolling 57 per cent of students (Manirakiza et al., 2019, p. 299; Ministry of Education Rwanda, 2019). As state-funded organisations, the public institutions – the University of Rwanda, Rwanda Polytechnic, and the Institute of Legal Practice and Development – are required to align their research and teaching with the national development agenda (Twiringiyimana, Daniels and Chataway, 2021, p. 9). There are also a couple of notable parastatals: the sector is regulated by the Higher Education Council, an independent government agency that reports to the Ministry of Education. And in 2017 the National Council for Science and Technology was established to govern science, technology innovation and research, and to manage the National Research and Innovation Fund; it reports to the Government of Rwanda and is co-chaired by the Minister of Education.

The University of Rwanda has been the subject of less academic scholarship than most of the other flagship universities in this book. This is partly explained by its recent formation: the University of Rwanda is a new flagship. However, the university is indelibly shaped by its predecessor institutions, and these too have received less attention than regional counterparts such as Makerere and Addis Ababa. The following chapters collectively analyse the engagement activity of all ten flagships – despite their deep roots in particular places and contexts, they nonetheless have a great deal in common.

CHAPTER 4

BLURRING AND BRIDGING OF GEOGRAPHIC SCALES

We now turn to the engagement activity presented in the ten flagship university strategic plans shown in Table 3. This chapter begins by situating the strategic plan as an object of analysis within academic inquiry and within sub-Saharan Africa. It then explores how the ten strategies were developed and the implications for local development activity, before looking at different geographic scales of activity.

Table 3 Flagship university strategies analysed

Flagship university	Period covered	Title (citation)	Notes
Addis Ababa University	2020-2030	A Ten-Year Strategic Plan (Addis Ababa University, 2020)	
Makerere University	2020-2030	Unlocking the Knowledge Hub in the Heart of Africa (Makerere University, 2020)	
University of Cape Town (UCT)	2016-2020; 2020-2030	Distinguishing UCT: A Strategic Planning Framework (UCT, 2016); Vision 2030: Unleash Human Potential for a Fair and Just Society (UCT, 2021b)	
University of Ghana	2014-2024	Strategic Plan (University of Ghana, 2014)	
University of Ibadan	2015-2020	Agenda for the Accelerated Development of the University of Ibadan through Consolidation and Innovation (Olayinka, 2015); My Stewardship as Vice-Chancellor (2015-2020): Partial Listing of Fundamental Achievements (Olayinka, 2020)	Olayinka (2020) is a summary of activities, rather than a forward-looking strategic plan
University of Mauritius	2015-2020	Strategic Plan (University of Mauritius, 2015)	
University of Namibia	2019-2024	Strategic Plan (University of Namibia, 2019)	
University of Rwanda	2018-2025	Strategic Plan (University of Rwanda, 2018b)	
University of Zambia	2018-2022	Strategic Plan (University of Zambia, 2018)	

Flagship university	Period covered	Title (citation)	Notes
University of Zimbabwe	2019-2025	Educating to Change Lives (University of Zimbabwe, 2019a)	Full version seen by author but not in public domain; only extracts published on university website quoted in analysis

The analysis of strategic plans in academic inquiry

Strategic plans offer significant opportunities for analysis. They can be a 'way of knowing' what should be done, who should do it, why it should be done, and how, across complex organisations (Bryson, Crosby and Bryson, 2009, p. 201). They present insight into the priorities, plans, and values of an institution, and can reflect and in turn reproduce wider societal or international discourses.

However, the limitations of strategic plans necessitate a critical approach when we handle them, and their often idealised and politicised nature requires us to be careful of accepting statements at face value. An institution-wide plan may reflect the views of a single department or a few individuals, or a compromise reached by omission and obfuscation. A strategy may have been crafted independently by the university, or shaped by the spoken or unspoken wishes of government or funding bodies. Marginalised groups may be excluded, and the process of forming plans can be top-down and non-participatory – even when the planning process is ostensibly open to all staff and students; different stakeholders will have varying degrees of influence (Falqueto et al., 2020).

Plans may bear little resemblance to the lived reality of those people whom the plan is intended to serve. They are sometimes hard to access or simply unavailable, and can quickly become dated. On-the-ground reality can quickly diverge from carefully laid plans as opportunities arise and crises hit. As Addie (2019b, p. 1618) notes, although strategic plans can form the basis of rigorous comparison, 'universities act through the negotiation of policies and the mobilisation of multiple (not necessarily coherent) channels, not through plans themselves'.

Strategies are rarely followed by a comprehensive and objective evaluation. Nevertheless, strategic plans can still tell us something about how an institution works, its plans, and – in particular here – how flagship universities view and approach external engagement activity.

Figure 2 shows some questions asked of flagship plans in this chapter, mapped onto the process of producing ('upstream'), publishing, and then using ('downstream') a strategic plan, although it should be noted that the downstream components largely fall outside of the scope of this study.

```
┌─────────────────────────────────────────────┐
│                   Upstream                     │
│                                                │
│         Who are the decision makers?           │
│       How participative is the process?        │
│           Who approves the plan?               │
└─────────────────────────────────────────────┘
                        │
                        ▼
┌─────────────────────────────────────────────┐
│                Plan published                  │
│                                                │
│            What is the purpose?                │
│           Who is the audience?                 │
│            What are the aims?                  │
└─────────────────────────────────────────────┘
                        │
                        ▼
┌─────────────────────────────────────────────┐
│                 Downstream                     │
│                                                │
│       How is the plan disseminated?            │
│  How is it understood, translated, implemented?│
│       Is the plan monitored or evaluated?      │
└─────────────────────────────────────────────┘
```

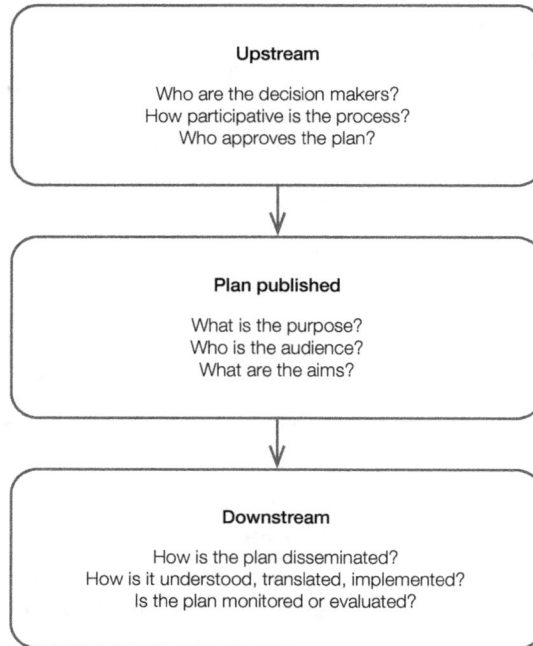

Figure 2 Interrogating a university strategic plan

In line with the broader literature on local university engagement, previous studies of university strategic plans mostly focus on North American and European institutions. Gaffikin and Perry (2009, p. 130) examined how the strategic plans of a sample of large US research universities have been shaped by discourses of globalisation, including whether planning documents illustrate a shift towards social engagement, entrepreneurial research, and a 'strategic turn' to managerial forms of administration. Ehlenz (2018) assessed the anchor role of 22 urban universities in the US. Addie (2019b) examined the institutional and spatial strategies of universities in London and New York, comparing the organisational structures, spatial orientations, and ways of operating in each city. There are a couple of studies that look beyond the Global North. This book complements work by Bekele and Ofoyuru (2021) and Bekele, Cossa and Barat (2021), examining the strategic plans of regional African organisations and a broad set of African universities to understand university-society relationships. Ngwana (2003) looked at the formation of the 1998–2003 University of Buea strategic plan, and welcomed the role of the Cameroonian Ministry of Higher Education as a referee rather than a player in the process. More recently, Stensaker et al. (2019) examined the strategies of 78 universities in 33 countries, including eight in sub-Saharan Africa, and found similar strategic positioning within status groupings: high-ranked, medium-low ranked, and unranked universities. As such, globalisation and internationalisation have not led to a single form of homogenised strategy, but a 'snakelike procession' of unranked universities aspiring towards medium-low ranked institutions, and medium-low ranked universities towards high-ranked ones.

Strategic plans as 'key sites of institutional discourse'

A strategic plan has a specific purpose, audience, and aims. It also has a history, both in terms of the process of authoring that may have involved multiple, competing authors with diverging or overlapping interests, and antecedents – other documents, conversations, and events that knowingly or unknowingly, explicitly or implicitly, shaped the plan. Strategic plans are a rich source of information on policies and practices that can tell a story of institutional interests and, especially when considered collectively, the broader, structural forces that shape these. As Bowen (2009, p. 29) points out, documents such as strategies provide data on the context within which research participants operate, as well as bearing witness to past events. Strategies are a static compromise emerging from an active process of development, or, according to Gaffikin and Perry (2009, p. 138), 'key sites of institutional discourse'. The lenses of purpose, audience, and aims help us to see why strategic plans are – in the words of Krippendorff (2010, p. 234) – valuable 'vehicles of communication', offering us a window into flagship universities and their local engagement activity.

The *purpose* of a strategic plan, taken at surface value, is to provide an indication of priorities, or at least a signal of what is considered important or necessary. Strategic plans are ways to balance institutional ambitions (to attract international students, for example) and external expectations (such as accountability for public money) (Drori and Honig, 2013, p. 345; Stensaker et al., 2019, p. 541). Beyond this, and with emphasis on the *strategic*, plans can be 'interactive, proactive, selective, and visionary' (Albrechts, Balducci and Hillier, 2016, p. 16). They may aim to establish new initiatives or to respond to external circumstances. The appointment of a new vice chancellor may result in an attempt to distance the institution from the previous regime, to restructure, or to build on recent achievements. Most are mandatory: although the form and content will vary, national ministries or higher education bodies require planning documents from universities, usually along a five- to ten-year horizon, and any funding is usually predicated on an acceptable medium-term plan. International funders – a multilateral body such as the World Bank financing an Africa Higher Education Centre of Excellence (ACE) at the University of Ghana, or a national donor such as SIDA, Sweden's government agency for development, funding a five-year programme at Addis Ababa University – also require strategic plans, sometimes bespoke, but usually referencing broader organisational frameworks or adapted from a core university planning document.

In many cases, the *audience* is ostensibly the university community: staff and students. For staff, in particular leaders charged with implementation, strategic plans are 'signposts' to shape subsequent decisions (Mastop and Faludi, 1997, p. 815). It would be naïve, however, to consider the academic community as the only audience. The audience is rarely made explicit, but it can help to ask why the strategy was written, and how it might reflect power and decision-making structures. A university strategy may be aimed at the head of state, or the university council (sometimes these are effectively one and the same). A version of the university strategy written for SIDA might be aimed at senior leaders at the agency, or it might be a reflection of an implicit understanding between the university and the agency that the real audience is the Swedish government, or even the Swedish electorate. A strategy with one eye on attracting World Bank funding may reflect the norms of the ACE programme – norms that are shaped by wider international discourses around higher education and economic development.

Aims are closely related to both purpose and audience. These are likely to be both internal and external: to measure and guide the activity of staff within the university (as above), and to inform and persuade external audiences that the university and its activity have merit (in order to increase funding, expand reach and remit, change direction, or simply to ensure survival). Universities are large, complex institutions: a plan may aim to bind an organisation together, and provide a degree of coherence, especially in the face of unforeseen challenges (Chance and Williams, 2009, p. 38). In principle, an internal audience can be judged on how they delivered according to the plan, and an external audience can hold the organisation to account. As such, although the document itself may be a form of static compromise, it can continue to be subject to interpretation and contestation. A further aim may be to inculcate trust in the organisation – evidenced, perhaps, by judicious use of positive imagery and professional design, and by the considered use of language. The extent to which a strategy is publicly available may also reveal information on the aims and audience.

Strategic plans in sub-Saharan Africa

Fredua-Kwarteng (2020) critiques the strategic planning document as an imported management technique from the North, imposed on sub-Saharan African universities in the 1990s. He identifies two reasons for this: first, a requirement by the World Bank, who wanted the plan to be used as a basis for funding discussions between the university and the government and donors. Second, as part of a push for African universities to gain greater autonomy from the state. Fredua-Kwarteng suggests that the strategic plan, in its current form, is unsuited to African universities today because they do not have the distance from government and the freedom to design and enact their strategies. However, there is likely some wiggle room behind the scenes, as the actions and activities within strategic plans are wrangled into place as part of negotiations between university staff and government officials. The influence of the Global North is less contestable. This influence has been direct, for example, as documented by Ngwana (2003, p. 10) with the University of Manchester running workshops to develop the University of Buea strategic plan at a formative time for the institution – six years after it had been awarded full university status. The influence is also indirect: the very existence of a university strategic plan is the norm amongst most large universities in many countries around the world. Plans tend to fit a fairly standard profile: there is more similarity between the format of the University of Cape Town strategic plan and the University College London strategic plan than the composition of their student bodies, for example. The values of the entrepreneurial university model, whilst contested and subject to considerable variation between universities, have shaped this standardised model of the strategic plan, and are rooted in European and North American higher education systems (Stensaker et al., 2019, p. 541).

Yet strategic plans have taken on an outsized importance in many African flagship universities. Their launches are often glitzy affairs covered by the national press. A formal planning document has perhaps a higher status and broader significance within many African countries than in the UK or the US. For example, strategic plans carry great weight in Rwanda; a detailed strategic plan complements the top-down administrative structure and 'instinctive efficiency' in the country (Wrong, 2021, p. 387). Goodfellow and Smith (2013, p. 3193) express this nicely: 'the [city development] plan wields enormous influence: one interviewee even commented that "[we] are all impaled on the Master Plan"'. For African flagship universities, therefore, the contents of their strategic plans can help us understand their role in society, and the process that underpins their development sheds light on whose voice counts when planning the future.

Approaches to preparing strategic plans

On the surface, the process for constructing flagship university strategic plans (the 'upstream' component of Figure 2) appears remarkably similar. For the University of Rwanda plan, 'considerable inputs have been received from internal stakeholders ranging from senior managers, staff, students, and other stakeholders' to reflect national and international aspirations (2018b, p. 3). The Addis Ababa University plan is the result of 'extensive participation' from the university community (2020, p. 9). The perspectives of students, faculty, the government, and national and international organisations were gathered through focus group discussions and informed the intent statements (2020, p. 7), and then the plan was 'consolidated' through workshops and events with the university community and 'high level experts' (2020, p. 11). The University of Ghana (2014, p. 8) strategic plan draws upon several months of consultation with the leadership of the university and 'a good cross-section of stakeholders'. The University of Zimbabwe strategy is the result of 'comprehensive consultation' with a range of university stakeholders including industry, civil society and students (University of Zimbabwe, 2019b). The University of Zambia (2018, p. i) strategy was informed by feedback from a mid-term review of the previous plan, and then shaped by 'the university community'. And a foreword by the chair of the university council in the University of Namibia (2019, p. 6) strategic plan simply says the plan was developed in an 'inclusive and participatory manner'.

Given the centrality of planning documents in determining the activities and strategic direction of flagship universities in sub-Saharan Africa, it is important to examine the process by which they are constructed to understand the role of flagships in their local areas and the possible scope of local engagement. Most notably, the voice of the (non-university) local community and the broader public seem to be absent in consultation processes. Subtle differences also emerge between flagships, with implications for any activity which follows. The University of Ibadan strategic plan is the personal 'manifesto' of the then-incoming vice chancellor, setting out in intricate detail the priorities of his five-year tenure. Although it still draws on 'extensive consultation' with the university community – staff members submitted 'memoranda on how to reposition our dear institution … their various views were synthesised in order to produce a coherent picture' (Olayinka, 2015, p. 14) – the influence of an individual is more pronounced than in the other flagships.

Strategies that appear to be open and participatory can still be shaped by power structures. The UCT (2021b) plan is a high-level vision statement that is more abstract than its continental counterparts. It describes itself as a living strategy – 'an idea that is constantly reshaped in different parts of the organisation and that elicits an emotional and intellectual commitment across all sectors of our community', instead of the 'typical approach' of a document that ends up 'lost at the bottom of a website or forgotten in a drawer' (2021b, p. 1). University leaders emphasise consultation and participation through engagement events with academic, professional, administrative and support staff (Simon, 2020). However, questions should be asked about how truly representative these processes are. The process at UCT began in 2018 with the vice chancellor presenting the three pillars of the academic project at UCT – excellence, transformation and sustainability – to help shape discussions, as well as setting up the Futures Think Tank, led by the dean of the Faculty of Engineering & the Built Environment, to examine how the university could best adapt to meet societal challenges (UCT, 2021b, p. 4). As a result, the tone, starting points and direction have all been set from the top of the institution. When the foundations have been set by a figure as powerful as the vice chancellor, it is perhaps unlikely these will be fundamentally challenged. Although the student protests are acknowledged as an impetus for change, students do not appear to be part of these discussions, let alone local communities. The supposedly 'open' and 'consultative' process for formulating a university strategic plan is undermined by a senior leader setting 'loose themes' to begin the conversation, potentially closing down new ideas.

Others have had marked government influence. The Makerere University strategy states that it was developed by the University Council with input from stakeholders (2020, p. 2). However, commentators have noted that Makerere's strategic plan 'draws heavily' on the report of a presidential visitation committee (titled "Bringing the Future to the Present") (Kigotho, 2020). The committee was appointed by Ugandan President Yoweri Museveni, after he closed the university in November 2016 following staff and student strikes. The relationship between Makerere and the government illustrates the often circular dependence of flagships on their national leaders: lecturers at Makerere University went on strike because the government failed to pay them; students went on strike because they were not being taught; the government closed the university because of strikes; the government instilled a commission to look at challenges facing the university; the commission recommended that Makerere 'strengthen initiatives to explore diverse sources of revenue' – away from government funding (African Centre for Media Excellence, 2016; Rwendeire, 2017, p. xii). The majority of flagship strategies analysed in this book have a foreword provided by a government minister; it is likely that the majority will have been approved by government officials before publication.

As such, much of the debate and consultation that feeds into strategic planning is likely to be over nuance and detail, rather than broad aims and objectives, as these will be influenced largely by government or the senior leadership team – with little or no participation by local communities or the broader public. Whilst these documents may be more transparent and consultative than the previous model of strategic plan, which often emerged fully formed from the senior leadership team after extensive input from donor-funded consultants (Farrant and Afonso, 1997, p. 23), we cannot assume they are representative of the entire institution. However, there are differences between the plans, and Table 4 presents a model of the forms university strategic planning can take. Most of the flagship strategies analysed sit somewhere towards the nexus of the boxes, a scattering of points in the centre with small degrees of difference between them. UCT, for example, would be situated towards the bottom right, whereas the University of Ibadan is likely to sit towards the top left.

Table 4 Forms of university strategic planning

	DIRECTIVE AND PRESCRIPTIVE	OPEN-ENDED
TOP-DOWN PROCESS	Tight, centralised control; inflexible	To be translated into implementation plans; cascade down through organisation
WIDE CONSULTATION	Highly-detailed plans; complex implementation structures	Vision statements; aspirational

The process for implementing flagship university strategic plans (the 'downstream' component of Figure 2) also appears remarkably similar across institutions. For the University of Rwanda, the strategy is a framework to be translated into implementation plans at college, school, and departmental level (2018b, p. 4). Academic and business units within Addis Ababa University will be given 'maximum autonomy' to execute their strategic plans, but strong performance management systems will be in place (2020, p. 41). The University of Mauritius (2015, p. 1) plan is a 'guiding document' based on consultation with internal and external stakeholders. At the University of Namibia, corporate strategic objectives will be 'cascaded' into divisional business plans, which will in turn be 'cascaded' into annual management plans. Progress updates will be given to pro-vice chancellors monthly (2019, p. 9). Finally, personal scorecards will be developed for all staff members (2019, p. 37). At the University of Zambia, faculties and departments will construct their own plans to meet the objectives specified in the institutional strategy (2018, p. vi). The implementation of the plan's targets will be reported on a monthly and quarterly basis (2018, p. 53).

Again, understanding processes of implementation is important, with the degree of autonomy afforded to departments and faculties acting as an enabler for, or constraint on, local engagement activity. Whilst it is easy to dismiss staff scoreboards and monthly indicator reporting as managerialism or bureaucratic micromanagement, their form and function shape incentives to conduct new activity and to form new partnerships, and directly determine promotion criteria and career pathways. They are also intended to influence donors: the University of Zambia (2018, p. 5) encourages development partners who wish to work with the university 'to support those [activities] that are in line with the strategic directions'.

Geographic scales of flagship activity

All flagship university strategies discuss activity at the local level, albeit to different extents, as shown in Table 5. Similarly, all discuss their national and international activities and aspirations, with some crossover between the scales. Beyond this, however, the concept of place itself is not articulated in any detail. Occasionally, the definitions of scales changes between sections of the strategic plan – for example, when the University of Rwanda plan discusses regional development needs, these are presumed to mean the East African community on one page (University of Rwanda, 2018b, p. 13), and then the challenges facing Africa as a continent in another (University of Rwanda, 2018b, p. 11). Similarly, who constitutes the 'community' or 'communities' is rarely expanded upon, except to distinguish between the academic and non-academic community (for example, Addis Ababa University, 2020, p. 7), or the local versus the global community (Addis Ababa University, 2020, p. 47). However, some do discuss their city. These scales are considered in turn from the global to the local, together with some examples of where scales are blurred or joined.

Table 5 Local engagement activity within flagship university strategic plans

Flagship university	Local engagement activity in plan	
Addis Ababa University	12 strategic goals are identified: 'provide transformative and scholarly community engagement' is number four. Sections of the report detail community engagement and community service strategies.	•
Makerere University	Goal four (of four) is to become 'an engaged university with enhanced partnerships with industry, the community and international institutions'.	
University of Cape Town	The 2016-2020 framework lists 'social impact through engaged scholarship' (including the expansion of community and external partnerships) as goal five (of five). The draft 2030 Vision is much higher-level, with social engagement a 'cross cutting element'.	
University of Ghana	Little mention of local engagement except for developing a process for assessing and publishing the impact of community engagement and outreach programmes.	
University of Ibadan	16 priorities are elaborated in some detail: number 13 is 'Corporate Social Responsibility' to meet the needs of communities in the Ibadan region.	•
University of Mauritius	Sustainable community engagement is the fifth 'strategic direction' (of six).	
University of Namibia	There are five overarching themes, including 'community engagement, environmental sustainability and social relevance' (number four).	•
University of Rwanda	Strategic goal three (of eight) is 'responsible community engagement and networking'.	•

Flagship university	Local engagement activity in plan	
University of Zambia	Seven 'strategic directions' include 'promote community outreach and beneficial partnerships' (number three).	•
University of Zimbabwe	Each of seven strategic objectives has a set of outcomes driven from four areas: innovation, industrialisation, teaching and community outreach.	

• Includes indicators, targets and/or baseline figures for local/community engagement activity.

The quest for global recognition

Except for Addis Ababa University (2020, p. 29), none of the surveyed universities describe themselves as a 'flagship' institution. Many instead echo the University of Ibadan's aspiration to become a world-class university (Olayinka, 2015, p. 46). The University of Ghana (2014, p. 7) observes that 'it has become fairly standard for universities around the globe to claim a "world class" vision', before stating later in the same paragraph that the vision of the university is to become a 'World Class Research-Intensive University'. Even where flagship status is acknowledged, this is married to global ambition. Following the 'sparkling success' of the previous Addis Ababa University plan, which had the vision of the university being 'among the top ten pre-eminent graduate and research universities in Africa', the 2020–2030 plan adopts a more global goal: to be 'among the world class universities and one of the leading regional research universities by 2030' (Addis Ababa University, 2020, pp. 5–6). It will 'work aggressively' towards the internationalisation of its programmes (2020, p. 13).

The University of Rwanda aspires to be 'internationally recognised', and a 'globally engaged, competitive, and innovative research-driven university' (2018b, pp. 8–10). One way it proposes to achieve this is by prioritising 'research areas that advance the University as an internationally recognised University'. It is important to understand the decision-making process that will underpin this prioritisation: will areas already recognised in league table rankings be supported at the expense of emerging fields? Will neglected but potentially transformative subjects be dropped in favour of those championed by industry? What about research areas with strong local benefit but limited international appeal? The strategy does not make this clear.

Occasionally, the global visions of the university align with the goals of the national government. The University of Mauritius (2015, p. 1) refers to serving the global community alongside the developmental needs of the country. One proposed means is an Asia-Africa Knowledge Platform (2015, p. 14), complementing a national development aspiration to be a bridge between the two continents. Strong regional links with East African states are also seen as particularly important for the small island state.

Demonstrating national relevance

In keeping with their origins and historic role, Africa's flagship universities have a strong emphasis on their national relevance in their strategic plans. For the University of Ghana

(2014, p. 5), the priority is to 'step up its research profile extensively, and in the process meet the growing research needs of the country and region'. The plan notes that a new Office of Research Innovation and Development has led to significant increases in both external and internal funding for research. New partnerships with industry will help promote research in national priority areas (2014, p. 12). The University of Rwanda's vision and mission, research centres, and curricula will be aligned with Rwanda's development needs, determined by the national Vision 2020 plan and EDPRS2 (Economic Development and Poverty Reduction Strategy); the university is 'inextricably linked with the nation's development' (2018b, pp. 9–13). Addis Ababa University considers the contribution of staff to significant national economic, social and political affairs as a strength, citing an example of negotiations over the Grand Ethiopian Renaissance Dam. However, research outputs currently have 'limited impact' for national development (Addis Ababa University, 2020, p. 24). In the new plan, research priority areas will be updated to match the national development agenda (2020, p. 37). The mission and vision of Makerere University (2020, p. 5) focuses on being responsive to national and global needs, addressing the complex issues of the 'nation, region and Africa'. The plan is aligned with Vision 2040, Uganda's aspiration to achieve middle-income status within the next two decades (2020, p. 9). 'Knowledge and Technology Transfer Partnerships' are the vehicle for translating university research into national development (2020, p. 11), but greater involvement of university researchers in formulating government policy and setting up joint think tanks with government agencies are also mentioned (2020, p. 19).

In contrast with some of the other flagships profiled here, the University of Zimbabwe strategy is predominantly national in focus, with references to international status framed within national development aspirations and the goal of becoming an upper-middle-income country by 2030. The plan commits the university to the ambitious goal of contributing to at least 30 per cent of the advanced knowledge products, processes, goods and services in national industry and commerce (the current contribution is not specified) (University of Zimbabwe, 2019c). Across the border, the University of Namibia (2019, p. 8) has an early and explicit commitment in the opening line of its executive summary to 'redouble efforts to support government'. As with the University of Zimbabwe, international ambitions (in this case to be 'internationally robust and resilient') are a means of supporting national development (2019, p. 9). The university's mission statement focuses on achieving national and international development goals (2019, p. 14).

In countries that are relatively geographically small, such as Mauritius, a case can be made for conflating the local and national community outside the university. The University of Mauritius has plans to provide students with community service opportunities (University of Mauritius, 2015, p. 10), to act as a think tank for the country (2015, p. 16), and to respond to societal needs (2015, p. 8), sitting alongside 'sustainable community engagement' as a strategic direction (2015, p. 3). Objectives to 'provide services to communities living around the campus' (the types of service are not specified), to support the local community to develop sustainable solutions to problems they face, to include the voice of local communities in the university research agenda, and to measure the number of activities carried out benefiting the local community (2015, pp. 16–17), suggest that there is also a sub-national focus. However, this is framed as charitable activity directed at beneficiaries, rather a product of equal partnership. In addition, activities such as formal and informal courses, and the development of 'turn-key solutions for the communities', appear to mostly take place on campus rather than being embedded within the community (2015, p. 17).

Local and community engagement in strategic plans

There is evidence within strategic plans of a turn towards local and community engagement, but this remains an emergent focus. The University of Namibia (2019, p. 12) views 'insufficient engagement of communities in social projects' as an institutional weakness. Strategic objectives to help rectify this include strengthening sustainable community engagement, improving social relevance and increasing strategic social projects, and strengthening mechanisms for climate change mitigation and adaptation (2019, p. 17). The strategy states that there is an increasing international awareness 'that community engagement is an essential social responsibility of tertiary institutions', suggesting the influence of global narratives in shaping university planning in this area. As a result, the university 'will strive for social relevance in the community, by deploying scholarly expertise and resources to engage with communities within the context of reciprocal engagement and collaborative partnerships' (2019, p. 21). Weaknesses are also noted in other strategies. Addis Ababa University (2020, p. 9) aims for 'state of the art research and community engagement accomplishments', and observes that there is increasing societal demand for community services and partnership (2020, p. 15). However, staff currently make a 'low contribution' compared to the expectations of the community (2020, p. 25).

Other flagships approach the local from a different angle. For Makerere University (2020, p. 19), relations with industry are prioritised in discussions on engagement, and take a technology-first approach: the 'education and research agenda will be driven by the potential of the university to harness and diffuse emerging technology breakthroughs in fields such as robotics and artificial intelligence, big data, quantum computing and the Internet of Things, as well as Nano and biotechnology'. Following this, the employability of graduates depends upon being able to 'effectively harness new local and global opportunities as they emerge'. The importance ascribed to technology is reminiscent of the inclusive innovation strategies of some cities in the Global North, and similar critiques might be levelled here: that a focus on the 'new and exciting' instead of the 'effective and boring', and the search for technological fixes for complex social problems, is misplaced (Lee, 2020, p. 3). However, a sub-theme calls upon Makerere to prioritise the needs of the community near the university and to enhance community outreach programmes. Elsewhere, the University of Zimbabwe strategy 'adopts a radical departure' from the three traditional pillars of teaching, research and community service. Although these pillars remain, the chairman of council explains that two new pillars – innovation and industrialisation – will combine to form 'Education 5.0' to help transform the national economy (University of Zimbabwe, 2019b).

However, community outreach is an outcome that cuts across each of the seven strategic objectives (University of Zimbabwe, 2019a).

Three strategies discuss their city or city region. Addis Ababa University (2020, p. 16) makes several references to the capital city in a section on opportunities. The convenient geographic location, and the international organisations hosted in the city, are an asset (the city is the 'third diplomatic centre in the world' (2020, p. 29)). The 'massive infrastructural investment' in Addis Ababa means demand for expertise in architecture, construction, project management, public realm improvements, ICT, power, and financial management.[20] The City Administration of Addis Ababa is listed as a stakeholder with two main goals: serving as a link between the university and the local community, and working to solve staff housing issues (2020, p. 51). Second, the University of Zambia (2018, p. 6) emphasises its location in the heart of Lusaka, which 'presents opportunities for multi-sectoral cooperation and linkages'. The university needs to 'leverage' this location, together with the 'competitive advantage' of being the country's oldest university. Third, the University of Ibadan compares its host region unfavourably to Lagos ('the commercial capital of the country'), citing this as a weakness. The 'inability to secure consistent and sustainable support and engagement with Oyo and other state governments' is another weakness, but the possibility of strengthening these local relationships is seen as an opportunity (Olayinka, 2015, p. 54). In conclusion, while flagships recognise the importance of local and community engagement, the extent of focus and the approach taken varies, with some emphasising technology, others prioritising community needs, and a few highlighting the relative merits of their geographic locations.

The glonacal agency heuristic in practice

Although extensive theorising about the relationship between multiple scales of place has taken place in the academic field of regional and urban studies (see introduction), parallel work has quite independently taken place in the field of higher education studies. Marginson and Rhoades (2002) introduced their 'glonacal agency heuristic' to guide work in comparative higher education and help further understanding of how phenomena unfold, with an emphasis on looking beyond the nation state as the sole frame of reference.

> *One of our aims is to advance the significance of studying global phenomena. Yet we do not see such phenomena as universal or deterministic in their effects; thus, we also feature the continued significance of the national dimension. Further, as we do not see either global or national phenomena as totalising in their effects, we feature the significance of the local dimension. For these reasons, we construct the term, "glonacal".*
> *(Marginson and Rhoades, 2002, p. 288)*

---

20 More broadly, the burgeoning Ethiopian middle class has meant an expansion in higher education, accompanied by vast building projects. The government has linked this agenda to attempts to modernise the construction industry and bring it up to international standards, overseen by foreign experts. See GIZ (2016) for an example.

The use of 'agency' refers to both entities or organisations as an agency (the World Bank, a government agency or a university), and the ability to exercise agency, either individually or collectively – the framework explores how both manifestations of agency play out across the glonacal. The authors emphasise the non-hierarchical interplay and flows between the levels of place, and between the two forms of agency, and build several additional dimensions into the model (Marginson and Rhoades, 2002, p. 291). 'Reciprocity' refers to the two-way interactions of ideas and activity. 'Strength' references the availability of resources, and the force and size of activity and influence. 'Layers and conditions' are the historic structures on which this activity and influence is based, and which provide the means for interaction between the levels. Finally, the 'spheres of agency' and activity determine the geographical scope of activity and influence. In a paper published twenty years later, Marginson (2022, p. 1365) revisited the glonacal agency heuristic and noted that it has been used as the basis for higher education research, but that 'single-scale nation-bound methods still have a strong hold'. The paper integrated insights from human geography, echoing some of the discussions above and as such represents an interaction between the two academic disciplines (2022, p. 1371). It also reiterated the pitfalls of methodological globalism and methodological nationalism – the privileging of the global or national scale respectively, with the view that it ultimately determines what happens on the other scales – and called for these single-scale visions to be 'cleared away to bring a fuller geography of higher education to life' (2022, p. 1390).

We have seen how for the University of Mauritius, in part due to its home on a small island state, distinctions between the local, national, and international are blurred. A similar blurring takes place in Rwanda, another relatively (geographically) small state and where the University of Rwanda has a national footprint. The university wants to become 'more accessible to non-academic communities' (University of Rwanda, 2018b, p. 15). It will create opportunities for staff and students and the wider community to contribute to capacity development aligned to Rwanda's development agenda – a statement made in the community engagement section, making no distinction between the local and the national. Occasionally, a more deliberate bridging between scales takes place, and sometimes within the same document: the University of Rwanda (2018b, p. 16) strategy makes clear the link between local and global. For example, the university 'will promote international perspectives by implementing teaching strategies that make explicit and ongoing connections between local experience and global discourses'. Others also connect the two scales. The University of Zambia (2018, p. vi) will develop curricula that are 'local in nature but with a global orientation'; Olayinka (2015, p. 24) discusses how strategic research at the University of Ibadan must contribute to local, national and global development, and become a university that is – in phrasing reminiscent of any UK Russell Group institution – 'locally relevant, nationally pre-eminent and globally competitive' (2015, p. 36).

Students are also a conduit for bridging the local and global. Both the vision and the mission of the University of Rwanda are channeled through graduates (in the vision to build 'a more just and sustainable society locally, nationally and globally') and students (in the mission to, amongst other things, transform 'communities through finding solutions') (University of Rwanda, 2018b, p. 7). Students will, the university promises, be prepared to serve communities and country (2018b, p. 9). More generally, Makerere University (2020, p. 13) calls on its students to be local, national and global citizens.

For the UCT (2021b, p. 5), there is no explicit focus on the local, but 'transformation' and 'social engagement' are cross-cutting themes. The university will put in place policies to 'enable, support and recognise civic engagement by staff and students' (2021b, p. 10), but 'civic engagement' is not defined. UCT will 'embrace local knowledge' and 'forge strong social partnerships with local communities' (2021b, p. 14). The previous 2016-2020 UCT strategy had objectives to expand community partnerships and the number of staff who engage with community-based organisations, to support the aspirations and development challenges of community-based organisations, and to offer practical projects with 'external constituencies' as part of the curriculum (UCT, 2016, p. 15). In a shift in focus, the current UCT (2021b) strategy recognises that the institution has 'struggled with its own identity', its colonial history, and its contradictory history during apartheid (2021b, p. 6). It chooses to spell Africa in its pre-colonial form ('Afrika') to 'validate the global character of the local in the 21st century', and orients itself as a global university in Africa. In doing so, it seeks to engage with societal challenges 'in their local manifestations and global implications' (2021b, p. 7). The impression is an institution uncomfortably aware of both its relative global prestige and its history, and seeking to root itself within the region. Thus the region becomes the focal point, rather than the local or global, and the university acts as a lens to promote African insights for a global audience, and make global knowledge relevant to Africa (2021b, p. 14). The intersection of different, 'glonacal', scales of place in African flagship strategies supports the assertion of Marginson (2022, p. 1390) that a single-scale view of higher education is insufficient to capture the totality of activity.

Universities and scales of place

For universities, the local, the national and the international (the 'glonacal') are often interconnected and interdependent – and sometimes in tension – and through the process of global engagement, universities represent their locality. Collinge and Gibney (2010, p. 386) suggest that university leaders face new complexities as a result of representing places rather than organisations: outcomes are difficult to measure, they lead initiatives without formal power but with responsibility, and they must accommodate the views of historically marginalised groups and organisations (such as social enterprises).

Somewhat paradoxically, it can be more difficult for universities to represent their locality within a city or a region than internationally, when they coexist with other universities or higher education providers. Where there are more than one or two universities, starting conversations with city leaders and building partnerships towards an agreed goal is a complex undertaking, particularly in a globally-integrated city where university leaders have to fight especially hard to be heard in a congested governance arena (Addie, 2016, p. 6). This raises fundamental questions about how universities should work together across and within areas – questions further complicated by competition (for students and funding), and national policy contexts that seek to build internationally-competitive knowledge economies (Naidoo, 2011, p. 41). These questions are pertinent in sub-Saharan Africa given the proliferation of institutions over the past half-century, and especially so for flagship universities, who have an outsized influence over national higher education sectors.

These relationships are further complicated by mixing what Goddard, Kempton and Vallance (2013, p. 58) call 'transactional' relationships with civic partnerships – the former including matters such as estate management. They advise keeping the two separate so any disagreements arising from one sphere do not negatively affect relations as a whole. But at a more basic level, there are often significant cultural and mission-related differences between university leaders and local or city leaders, with one side finding it difficult to understand the drivers or even the terminology of the other (Goddard, Kempton and Vallance, 2013, p. 57; Christopherson, Gertler and Gray, 2014, p. 214). However, whilst leadership decisions can give an indication of the strategic direction of universities and cities and their willingness and desire to cross different scales of place, the bulk of the interaction between universities and their place will take place at a lower level – between staff, students, the public, businesses and officials – adding to the complexity of the interaction but also potential breadth of impact.

Many universities have international links through staff and student recruitment, networks of alumni and researchers, membership of international bodies and organisations, the formation of branch campuses and international partnerships, and departments focused on global relations and the politics, history or development of specific regions of the world. In turn, universities can help internationalise their region (OECD, 2007, p. 16) and act as global gateways for attracting inward investment (Brown, 2022). Universities are simultaneously global players whilst significantly affecting their local environment; they operate on 'multiple and overlapping territories' and the challenge is to mobilise these connections to benefit the local area (Chatterton and Goddard, 2000, p. 478).

It is helpful to remind ourselves how different scales of place can coexist. Paasi and Metzger (2017, p. 9) recognise that the region is a 'flexible, malleable and mutable object of analysis'. Allen and Cochrane (2007) go a step further and propose that regions are political constructs.

> *the governance of regions, and its spatiality, now works through a looser, more negotiable, set of political arrangements that take their shape from the networks of relations that stretch across and beyond given regional boundaries. The agencies, the partnerships, the political intermediaries, and the associations and connections that bring them together, increasingly form 'regional' spatial assemblages that are not exclusively regional, but bring together elements of central, regional and local institutions. In the process … a more fluid set of regional political relationships and power-plays has emerged that call into question the usefulness of continuing to*

> *represent regions politically as territorially fixed in any essential sense. (Allen and Cochrane, 2007, p. 1163)*

As such, actors such as central government are not bodies that sit over or apart from regions, but are entangled in regional governance structures. Applied to higher education, the international activities of an urban university, for example, are very much part of that city region, if we are willing to look beyond the city as a purely geographical concept. As Addie (2016, p. 4) observes, universities are 'implicated in the global extension of urbanisation processes that, alongside the expansion and fragmentation of metropolitan space, defy the reduction of "the city" to an administrative unit or "the urban" to the local scale'.

There is therefore a clear divide between viewing the city, or the region, or the city region, as an inter-spatial concept that is both local and inherently international, and as an administrative unit that merely forms a constituent part of a greater whole. Officials governing the local and the regional will continue to be constrained by serving their fixed, territorial constituency, with the global being primarily a policy concern. Higher education has no such fixed constituency, and needs to 'define its sphere of influence in a flexible way' (OECD, 2007, p. 4).

Universities can simultaneously engage with multiple scales of place, and arguably this is most evident in cities, which themselves – owing to the dense network of institutions, people and businesses within them – draw on the international and shape the national, and are in turn moulded by both. To echo Goddard (2009), universities can be locally rooted and internationally engaged.

CHAPTER 5

WHAT DETERMINES ENGAGEMENT ACTIVITY?

This chapter explores how local engagement is measured in university strategic plans, and what this activity tells us about the role of flagship universities in society – recognising at the same time that there is an important distinction between a plan and the reality of its use in practice. The chapter finishes with a discussion on how flagships face difficult decisions and tensions as they plan for the future.

Implementation plans for local engagement activity

Four institutional strategies – Addis Ababa University (2020, p. 72), the University of Rwanda (2018b, p. 24), the University of Zambia (2018, p. 60), and the University of Namibia (2019, p. 32) – have numerical targets and, in some cases, baseline figures for local and community engagement activity. The University of Ibadan proposes performance indicators, but with no target figures attached (Olayinka, 2015, p. 266) (Table 5 shows those strategies with indicators for local or community engagement activity). The detail of these institutions is explored below. However, it is worth noting that the existence of implementation plans for five of the ten surveyed universities suggests a level of institutional capacity and commitment within those universities to local engagement activity (whilst recognising the possibility that flagships without such plans may have developed them separately, and those with targets and indicators may later change or ignore them). Others, such as the University of Ghana (2014, p. 28), want to develop a process for assessing the impact of community engagement programmes, and this may feature in a future strategy.

More broadly, a university – especially one as complex as a flagship – needs to have a mature administrative infrastructure in place to support an effective implementation plan for local engagement activity. Some do not yet have the capacity or capability, in much the same way as some flagship universities outside of this study do not have a strategic plan. A couple of flagships with implementation plans for local engagement activity touch on this issue more broadly. Addis Ababa University (2020, p. 18) bemoans the inability to fully utilise its alumni to attract resources and new partnerships, an ability predicated on an effective system for tracking graduates. The University of Zambia (2018, p. 11) strategic plan states that whilst the university conducts a lot of research, 'most of it is not documented/captured/attributed'. As we will see, this has implications for the University of Zambia: it recognised that it has a public image problem, to which it is responding by borrowing from the business playbook and developing a Corporate Social Responsibility policy to try to address.

Goals, indicators, targets, and baseline data

At the University of Rwanda, interventions target the 'primary occupation' in Rwandan communities with the intention of maximising the benefit of university activity. For example, goals include establishing a veterinary clinic at the Nyagatare Campus, opening model farms in the Eastern Province to showcase irrigation and agricultural mechanisation, and launching an animal feed manufacturing firm (University of Rwanda, 2018b, p. 24). Table 6 shows an extract from the 'Responsible Community Engagement and Networking' section of the implementation plan; in common with other flagships, the minimal baseline data for this suggests these are new areas of focus.

Table 6   Excerpt showing targets for the 'Promote community outreach activities' strategic priority area from the University of Rwanda strategic plan

Key performance indicator	Baseline (2017-18)	Target 2018/19 year 1	Target 2019/20 year 2	Target 2020/21 year 3	Target 2021/22 year 4	Target 2022/23 year 5	Target 2023/24 year 6	Target 2024/25 year 7
No. of community outreach programmes and activities	12	22	32	42	52	62	72	82
No. of identified and addressed community needs	0	22	32	42	52	62	72	82
No. of seminars organised to share research findings with the community	0	21	21	21	21	21	21	21
No. of beneficiaries	0	22 groups of people	32 groups of people	42 groups of people	52 groups of people	62 groups of people	72 groups of people	82 groups of people

Taken from the Responsible Community Engagement and Networking Strategic Goal 3 in the implementation plan (University of Rwanda, 2018b, p. 34).

In the Addis Ababa University (2020) plan, community engagement is distinct from *scholarly* community engagement. Engagement activities are reciprocal and 'designed to impart growth and development both for AAU and community partners' (2020, p. 47). The university plays the role of facilitator, promising to ensure appropriate governance structures for continued community engagement, encouraging academic units to assess community needs and respond accordingly, and ensure the 'efficient utilisation' of resources for community engagement. In other words, activity itself and the detail of engagement is devolved within the institution. Elsewhere in the plan, the 'incomplete devolution of power to lower level units as a result of insufficient accountability and enforcement mechanisms, and poor chain of command in decision making' is identified as a weakness: addressing this is therefore an important precondition for scaling up local engagement activity (2020, p. 18). A quality audit framework for community engagement activities will also be developed (2020, p. 101). For scholarly community engagement, Addis Ababa University will support female leaders to help achieve gender balance in public office, increase consultancy and commissioned research activity, and maintain a store of critical national data (2020, pp. 47–48).

The Addis Ababa University plan has a rich set of targets within the goal of providing transformative and scholarly community engagement, although these are high-level (2020, pp. 72–74). Some have an explicit place focus: to start satellite community projects (baseline: one; target number of satellite projects in operation in five years' time: 30). Within five years, the university aims to have 20 active community engagement centres, from a baseline of zero. Importantly, the university has targets for capacity building: 1,000 external and 5,000 AAU staff community engagement providers to be trained over the next five years. All staff should report being engaged in professional community services in five years' time – a proportion increasing by 20 per cent each year (from a baseline of zero). There will be 100 research outputs 'deliverable to the community' in the same timeframe, up from a baseline of ten. There are also metrics around identifying sources of finance and the number of funding applications prepared – it is unclear the extent to which community engagement activity is conditional on additional external funding.

The University of Ibadan lists some specific local projects that will be supported: a Women's Law Clinic established by the Faculty of Law in 2007 (where staff and students help disadvantaged women in Ibadan for free – 'the only specialised law clinic in Nigeria and perhaps in Africa' (Olayinka, 2015, p. 246)), and supporting students to teach in local deprived secondary schools in the summer holidays (Olayinka, 2015, p. 242). The university will measure the number of active partnerships and projects with local communities (Olayinka, 2015, p. 266).

The University of Zambia (2018) plan includes targets for developing a community-based capacity building programme, and a Corporate Social Responsibility (CSR) policy. The university will, for example, have 13 tailor-made and community-based programmes rolled out per year by December 2020 (one assumes these are likely to have been impacted by COVID-19); there is a baseline of 13 programmes. The vice chancellor, deputy vice chancellor, and deans are responsible for delivering this target, and there is a budget of one million ZMW (around GBP 28,800, or ZAR 673,000, in September 2024). Example activities include 'Consulta[tions] with possible participants; Development of modules; Training' (University of Zambia, 2018, p. 60) – it is assumed these are activities which lead to the formation of programmes, rather than the content of the programmes themselves, again suggesting a devolution of the detail within the institution. There will also be 15 CSR programmes by December 2020, also with a budget of one million ZMW; the baseline is undefined (2018, p. 59). An underpinning assumption for the plan as a whole is that local communities will be willing to work with the university (2018, p. 49); given the negative public perception reported in the strategy, this willingness is not necessarily to be taken for granted.

Under a strategic objective to strengthen sustainable community engagements, the University of Namibia (2019, p. 32) will measure the number of 'successful community engagements'. Although the baseline figure is blank, formulae for targets for 2019–2021 and 2022–2024 appear to draw on a forthcoming baseline figure: '(3B+50)' and '2(3B+50)+50' respectively. Strategic initiatives to drive this forward include to 'encourage outreach activities to strengthen relations with the community', and 'ensure service learning activities are undertaken within communities'. Other strategic initiatives have baseline data: under 'Improve Social Relevance and Increase Strategic Social Projects', the number of beneficiaries has a 2018 baseline of 561, a target of 870 beneficiaries between 2019 and 2021, and a target of 1,270 beneficiaries between 2022 and 2024.

In strategic plans with numerical goals, targets are linear, increasing by a similar number or percentage each year – for example in Table 6, above. They are not exponential or logarithmic, either of which could – in theory – be the case for a university starting local activity from a low base. It takes time to build a foundation for community engagement, but then a critical mass is reached and activity rapidly increases (exponential growth). Alternatively, when starting activity, the university finds there is pent-up demand, and the number of activities and people reached rapidly increases, until demand begins to be met, and growth slows (logarithmic growth). Patterns of growth will change from place to place, and if the universities with targets publish their progress it may be possible to gain a crude understanding of these patterns. Or, as is perhaps more likely, the reality of engagement will be somewhat messy and fail to conform to a pattern. Above all, however, we need caution over the limitations of targets and – in the words of Söderström, Paasche and Klauser (2014, p. 308) – the 'technocratic fiction' that any quantitative measure can replace knowledge, interpretation and specific thematic expertise.

Factors determining engagement activity

Africa's flagship universities are subject to considerable resource constraints, and are shaped by national and international policies and politics. These factors shape the extent to which they are willing and able to conduct local engagement and community work, the geographic scales within which flagships position themselves and their activities, and the traits of flagships themselves. Some of these factors are detailed in the universities' strategic plans, in particular financial constraints and the need to diversify sources of income away from government funding.

The University of Ghana (2014, p. 5) strategy discusses expected changes in how the university is funded, given shifts in the relationship between the university and the government and growth in services beyond teaching, in particular research. Government funding has fallen from more than 90 per cent of the budget to 55 per cent in a decade (2014, p. 6). Reliance on government funding is 'a liability'; dependence on fees will grow (but to no more than 60 per cent of the budget (2014, p. 22)). At the same time, the university takes a long-term view and recognises the need to maintain its land and physical assets 'for centuries to come' (2014, p. 6). The university owns a 'significant amount of land and property beyond the traditional physical boundaries of the university', and a database will be created to manage these assets (2014, p. 24).

Makerere University (2020, p. 21) discusses the need to grow and diversify income streams, and to reduce dependence on government funding by at least 30 per cent. For the University of Mauritius (2015, p. 19), more 'entrepreneurial activity' and consultancy contracts are a path to diversified income. At the University of Zambia (2018, p. viii), more revenue is needed 'for the survival of the institution' – competitive fees, consultancy work, investments, and partnerships are identified. This is a 'daunting' task (2018, p. 6). At the time of publication, a third of income was from government grants (2018, p. x). To break even, student numbers would need to increase from 25,000 to 45,000, but the strategy acknowledges this increase is unrealistic given the infrastructure of the university (2018, p. 15). As with the University of Ghana, the plan notes the 'prime land' owned by the university and available for development through public-private partnerships (2018, p. 10).

State funding for education at the University of Namibia has also decreased, and the university is keen to diversify funding to reduce reliance on government grants and tuition fees (University of Namibia, 2019, p. 18). The university plans to commercialise intellectual property and assets through a commercial entity called Inceptus. The University of Ibadan also seeks to reduce dependence on government funding. In addition to more consultancy, the vice chancellor seeks to generate more internal revenue though commercial ventures, led by a wholly owned umbrella company, UI Ventures Limited (Olayinka, 2015, p. 84). Subsidiary companies include a petrol station, a bakery, hotels, security services, paper recycling, advertising, water, and honey. Some of these businesses provide training in entrepreneurship for students.

Non-financial factors also constrain possibilities for local engagement, notably the employability agenda. The pressure for flagships to be seen as producing graduates with the technical and social skills needed by employers in nationally important industries trumps community engagement and local development activity, and is often treated as a higher priority by university leaders.[21] This is likely a global phenomenon and mirrors the UK, for example, where newspaper coverage and the views of national politicians tend to focus on 'low value degrees' and the suitability of graduates for work rather than concerns over the relationship between universities and their local area (Phoenix, 2021). In response, Addis Ababa University

---

21 The engagement and employability agendas intersect when universities work with industry to refresh the curriculum and provide learning opportunities for students, or students are supported to set up, for example, a social enterprise in the community. That the two agendas could reinforce each other is missing from the strategies.

(2020, p. 13) will admit a 'manageable' number of students, and prioritise the employability of its graduates, given the weakness of graduate employability in the past (2020, p. 20). For Makerere University (2020, p. 19), greater collaboration with industry and stronger curricula is the route to better employability outcomes, with graduates able to 'harness technology breakthroughs' to meet labour market needs (2020, p. 13). The University of Mauritius (2015, p. 5) will consult regularly with industry to increase the employability of its graduates. The University of Zambia (2018, p. 20) recognises that industry sees the university's graduates as 'not fully equipped'. The University of Namibia (2019, p. 8) draws on international narratives such as the fourth (and fifth) industrial revolution to inform academic programmes, referencing the World Economic Forum's 2016 report on the topic. And the University of Rwanda (2018b, p. 13) emphasises meeting the needs of the 'national and global workforce'.

Three final factors are worth mentioning. First, feedback received by the University of Zambia (2018, p. 14) revealed a negative public perception of the university. The strategy therefore calls for 'a need to deliberately develop a programme for changing the corporate image of the University'. Public perceptions are likely influenced by the discourse on graduate employability, but will extend beyond this to considerations of societal relevance more generally. Second, and again drawn from the University of Zambia's (rather frank) strategy, the extent of independence and autonomy of institutions will determine local engagement activity. The University of Zambia (2018, p. 16) is 'influenced politically by all kinds of political players', with members of the university council viewed as representing interest groups rather than the best interests of the university. The strategy calls for building a 'politically neutral and academically focused and liberal institution'. Third, a few strategies mention, albeit briefly, the Sustainable Development Goals (SDGs), with implications for university activity (Chapter 2). For example, the University of Rwanda (2018b, p. 8) will 'engage with' the SDGs, and Addis Ababa University (2020, p. 30) views the SDGs as an institutional opportunity and will align activity to the goals, alongside national and African Union agendas.

Marketisation and public roles in strategic plans

Flagship universities have characteristics in common, influenced in part by the forces and constraints that define their role. These in turn shape, facilitate, and limit local development activity. Some of these traits are visible in strategic plans and are described below. Two rough groupings emerge: one that suggests the influence of the marketisation and corporatisation of higher education, and another that pulls away from this, asserting the unique public role of the flagship as embodied in its founding role.

Pressures to marketise and corporatise

The need to diversify sources of funding compels flagship universities to seek new opportunities and new means of framing existing activity. In relation to local engagement activity, there are four ways this manifests itself within strategic planning. First, the reframing of some or all local and community development activity as Corporate Social Responsibility, borrowing the terminology of the private sector. The University of Ibadan lists Corporate Social Responsibility as a priority, particularly in the Ibadan region (Olayinka, 2015, p. 20). Engagement activities will be university-wide and 'supported with necessary logistics and rewarded'. The vice chancellor recognises that the university has 'been particularly lucky in maintaining very cordial relationship with its host community since its establishment', but 'there is an urgent need to contribute more to the immediate environment as part of our societal relevance' (Olayinka, 2015, p. 242). The University of Zambia (2018, p. 13) acknowledges that it has not had a deliberate programme for community outreach to date. However, the strategy (2018, p. viii) lists community outreach and beneficial partnerships as a strategic direction, with goals including the development and implementation of community-based capacity building programmes and a 'corporate social responsibility policy'.

Second is the permeation of the language of *customers* and *stakeholders* from the world of business. The local community is listed as one of six external stakeholders of Addis Ababa University (2020, p. 31). In their stakeholder matrix the local community have a *low* revenue impact, a *medium* frequency of contact, but a *high* degree of influence, *high* extent of direct benefit from the service of the university, and a *high* degree of importance according to the university mandate. Other external stakeholders – students (who are also listed separately as customers), the public, other higher education institutions, the international community, and donors and alumni – have a lower designated degree of influence compared to the local community, although most have a bigger impact on revenue. For the University of Namibia (2019, p. 11), students are the 'primary customer', and employees, central government, regional and local authorities, and the community in general are 'secondary customers'. The government is identified as wanting 'research output and consultancy assistance' from the university, and communities want a positive impact on society. It is necessary to disentangle the terminology of the market and the marketisation of local engagement, such as prioritising income generating activities ahead of public service – a point we return to in the concluding section.

Third is the importance placed on consultancy. Addis Ababa University (2020, p. 47) recognises that foreign companies win large consultancy contracts in areas of university expertise – management, engineering, law, environment, health – due to the 'lack of [a] competent local workforce'. It wants to build capacity in 'high-end/high-tech' tasks to reduce this dependence on foreign firms. The university also wants to increase the share of big surveys and research projects it conducts, without crowding out smaller consultants. The University of Zambia (2018, p. 9) views 'abundant opportunities' from consultancy services, which are in higher demand after the liberalisation of the economy. The University of Ibadan already has a consultancy service unit which partners with private companies to bid for contracts – it 'competes favourably' with the likes of PricewaterhouseCoopers and KPMG (Olayinka, 2015, p. 84). University departments will be encouraged to engage in consultancy and collaboration with industry (Olayinka, 2015, p. 18).

Fourth, flagships are keen to cultivate new partnerships with industry. A major goal of the University of Zimbabwe is the creation of new companies and industries. The vice chancellor describes the university's role as 'the "Rails" upon which the "Wheels" of Socio-Economic Development (i.e. industry and commerce) move' (University of Zimbabwe, 2019d). The University of Zambia (2018, p. 8) acknowledges that it has 'not adequately attracted knowledge and experience from industry'. As such, there is a 'very weak link' between the university and industry (2018, p. 17).[22] Other universities talk of partnerships more broadly, and with less of a market-driven imperative. The University of Rwanda (2018b, p. 11) wants to build relationships with government, industry, communities, and other research groups. Partnerships with 'stakeholders' are planned to help implement 'sustainable community based inclusive initiatives' (2018b, p. 15). UCT (2021b, p. 9) describes how it will 'work collaboratively with local and international social actors'.

Asserting a unique public role

Flagship universities are pulled in multiple directions to both adapt to and transform their position in society, but also to maintain their public- and nation-serving roots. Although their capacity and resources are limited, and in some cases have been eroded over the decades, and although they are no longer the sole provider of knowledge and higher education in their countries, they have a unique weight. A clout they still yield in society, a product of their history, their size, and their geographic reach, and which manifests in four ways in terms of local engagement activity. First, flagships are brokers of, and contributors to, public debate. The University of Rwanda (2018b, p. 15) will 'deliver public knowledge programs to the community and ensure contribution to public debate on issues of public importance'. A key performance indicator for the University of Mauritius (2015, pp. 16–17) is the number of public lectures and talks on national issues hosted by the university. As such, 'contributing to public discourse in relevant domains' is identified as a means of community engagement. Sometimes, however, universities feel the need to reign in some of their more enthusiastic employees. Addis Ababa University (2020, p. 48) wants to reduce incidences of staff appearing on television and radio and speaking on topics outside their expertise, which raises 'credibility issues to the university'.

Second, flagship universities have a role as institutional mentors and leaders of the national education system, extending their influence into towns, rural areas and communities far from their primary campuses. Despite the prominence and near-unanimity of this role, only two flagships discuss this in their strategic plan, perhaps because of the considerable burden it entails in terms of staff time. However, the University of Ibadan discusses this as a priority area, drawing on its 'historical role to provide leadership to the Nigerian University System' (Olayinka, 2015,

---

22 In a further example of the influence of the private sector on higher education institutions, the University of Zambia (2018, p. 14) provides an excellent example of the jargon that businesses are sometimes lampooned for: 'In the global village, synergising based on establishing mutually beneficial partnerships has been embedded as a key strategy especially in multinational entities'.

p. 24). Aims include building more collaboration between universities, lobbying the government, and avoiding the national strikes that have debilitated Nigerian universities. Addis Ababa University (2020, p. 14) views the commitment of the Ethiopian government to support AAU as a 'university of universities so that AAU trains teachers for other new universities' as an opportunity.

Third, flagships have an extensive physical presence in their country. In some cases, this is a result of the university extending its footprint by establishing multiple campuses, and in other cases through a process of decentralisation from a single major hub. The University of Zambia (2018, p. 6) has undertaken an 'ambitious programme' of scaling up its presence in all provinces outside the capital 'in order to take its services to the people'. For the University of Namibia (2019, p. 12), a 'wide physical presence' across the country is a strength of the institution. Twelve university campuses and regional centres 'physically [transform] the surrounding environments, neighbourhoods, cities and regions through modern, state-of-the-art investments, construction, landscaping upgrades and social networking capacity which create employment opportunities, support the service industry and sustain local economic development' (2019, p. 21). Reflecting on the outcomes of its previous strategic plan, Makerere University (2020, p. 23) notes that the objective to decentralise programme delivery was partially successful: two campuses were established at Jinja and Fort Portal, but the latter was closed due to low enrolment. The University of Ghana (2014, p. 6) notes some progress has been made with the decentralisation of the university into four colleges, and the majority of operations will be further decentralised through the college system (2014, p. 20).

Fourth, flagships recognise the importance of indigenous knowledge. Addis Ababa University (2020, p. 36) will 'explore indigenous knowledge and wisdom, and integrate it with conventional knowledge for solving societal problems'; Makerere University (2020, p. 11) plans to increase the profile of indigenous research. This topic is revisited in Chapter 7.

Tensions between historic roles and new demands

We can see shifts in position over time in university strategic plans, as approaches evolve between planning cycles and individuals join and leave the senior leadership team. For example, the Makerere University plan, covering the 2020–2030 cycle, promises 'a distinct shift to increased graduate enrolment and knowledge production' (Makerere University, 2020, p. 11). The previous ten-year plan discussed a shift from outreach (with its 'patronage connotation') to knowledge transfer, partnership, and networking, recognising the knowledge that resides within communities, local businesses, and non-governmental organisations (Makerere University, 2008, p. 4). The current plan, however, reverts to using the terminology of community outreach (2020, p. 19). On the other side of the continent, Ibadan's vice chancellor reflects on changes in the Nigerian university system and notes the

> *lack of synergy between the historical role of the university (teaching, research, service) and the new paradigm (economic development); this is reflected in the weak impact on the immediate community in particular and the nation in general; low quality skills of graduates; and huge skills gap in the economy. (Olayinka, 2015, p. 250)*

Tensions between the new and the old, the historical role of the flagship and the demands made today of higher education systems, of a publicly funded university and one seeking to diversify its income, are in part exemplified by the advent of terminology such as corporate social responsibility to describe local engagement activity. Whilst the marketisation of higher education has been vilified by academics in both the Global North (for example Collini, 2003) and South (for example Mamdani, 2007), this shift in language is perhaps not as insidious as it first appears. The definition of CSR itself has evolved (Latapí Agudelo, Jóhannsdóttir and Davídsdóttir, 2019). This has happened alongside changes in expectations for the broader role of businesses in society – rather than quick-fix, public relations-friendly measures to repair a tarnished image, CSR has more recently been defined by Porter and Kramer (2011) as the generation of *shared value*: 'policies and operating practices that enhance the competitiveness of a company *while simultaneously* advancing the economic and social conditions in the communities in which it operates' (my emphasis). The important takeaway is not that universities are looking to industry to learn how to do local development – little in their plans suggests this is the case beyond adopting some business-jargon and focusing on KPIs (key performance indicators). Instead, flagships increasingly need to align their local development activity and historic public mission with efforts to diversify income and to ensure employable graduates (this might, of course, also have the helpful effect of improving their public image). These tensions lead to universities sitting somewhere between two contrasts: treating the community as a stakeholder in the university or as a passive beneficiary; a grey area between flagships seeking self-interested partnerships or altruistic but paternalistic relationships.

The 'entrepreneurial university' provides a ready model for flagships seeking financial autonomy. It also prompts difficult decisions over resource allocation and prioritisation – even if income streams other than student fees are relatively small at present. For example, should a university work with a relatively prosperous local community to provide enterprise training, perhaps involving students and generating a small sum of money, or should it instead donate staff time to improve food security for an impoverished community on the university's doorstep? Is it possible to somehow balance both without compromising teaching quality or staff wellbeing? A widely adopted definition of the entrepreneurial university closely resembles that of CSR: to 'maximise the potential of commercialising [university] knowledge while also creating value for society, without considering this as a threat to [the university's] academic values and traditional functions' (Cerver Romero, Ferreira and Fernandes, 2020, p. 3). This balancing act of looking for common ground and areas of alignment between the core mandate and generating money will inevitably lead to compromises: new partnerships may involve local actors, but will marginalise others who do not bring immediate value to the table.

Some universities are compartmentalising their activity, for example with an explicit commitment to consultancy. We have seen how Addis Ababa University treats community *engagement* as distinct from community *service*, with the former framed as a reciprocal activity also benefitting the university. The University of Zambia (2018, p. 4) strategy splits its community service activities into three categories: consultancy, outreach, and extension activities. Consultancy services are usually provided for government, civil society or the private sector. Outreach is 'on a partnership basis' with communities around particular needs. Extension services are offered to communities 'which require introduction to, or upgrading of, particular new knowledge and skills that enhance the development endeavours in their environment'. Others steer in one direction: as seen earlier, the University of Mauritius views the community more as a beneficiary than an equal partner; the University of Namibia (a newer institution) focuses on partnership.

There are additional tensions between goals, partly due to opaque conceptualisations of place and scales of activity within strategic plans. Given the purpose and nature of planning documents these tensions and the trade-offs and difficult decisions they imply are, unsurprisingly, not acknowledged or explored by universities, with the limited exception of some linkages made between the local and the global. Two examples demonstrate these tensions. Makerere's vice chancellor wants to transform the university into a 'research-led institution', and 'elevate our reputation in the international arena' (Makerere University, 2020, p. 7). Accordingly, 'world class research metrics will be used to evaluate scholarly activities', but this could be at odds with a statement on the same page to 'address emerging society needs' (2020, p. 11). Second, local engagement activity is largely absent from the University of Ghana (2014) strategic plan, with the nation and region taking centre stage alongside an emphasis on building capacity. The main reference to local activity is a commitment to developing a process for assessing and publishing the impact of all community engagement and outreach programmes at the university (2014, p. 28). The connection between local engagement and building capacity, diversifying funding, producing nationally relevant research, partnering with industry, and responding to the demand from African societies to 'do more' beyond teaching – all sentiments reflected in the University of Ghana plan – is not made.

Reflections on a plan

As noted at the outset of Chapter 4, most strategic plans do not receive a formal evaluation, even though they are often a critical document for steering the direction of an institution and the thousands of staff and students it houses. Some, such as UCT's 'living strategy', are designed (at least in theory) to be constantly reshaped, but the act of adapting to changing circumstances can simply mean original targets are removed or changed, leaving little visible public record of what worked and what did not.

In contrast, the University of Ibadan's strategic plan is markedly different and is presented as a personal agenda. It is also unique in that the vice chancellor published a reflection on his tenure, *My Stewardship as Vice-Chancellor (2015-2020): Partial Listing of Fundamental Achievements*

(Olayinka, 2020). It does not match neatly onto the original plan and does not form an evaluation *per se*, but it is a valuable example of how circumstances and crises – both large and small – mean the reality of running an institution is consumed by reactive damage control rather than executing detailed plans, pushing supposedly priority areas, such as community engagement, from the fore. One example is a protracted struggle over maintaining payroll for teachers of Staff Schools (presumably a campus-based school for children of university staff) after the federal government pulled its funding (an 'obnoxious policy') (Olayinka, 2020, p. 102). Another, shared by organisations around the world, was COVID-19. The university's response demonstrates another trait of the flagship university: the circulation of staff. A professor from the University College Hospital was appointed as deputy chairman of the Oyo State COVID-19 Task Force. The deputy vice chancellor (Research, Innovation and Strategic Partnerships) was appointed as team lead for Oyo State COVID-19 Decontamination and Containment; her team published post-lockdown guidelines on the containment of COVID-19 in the state (Olayinka, 2020, p. 107). Community service activity did, however, continue, and examples are given (Olayinka, 2020, p. 95). Notably, the university signed a memorandum of understanding with the federal and Oyo state governments on the Ibarapa programme. This rural health programme has its origins in the early 1960s, with funding from the Rockefeller Foundation and technical support from both the Liverpool School of Tropical Medicine and the London School of Hygiene and Tropical Medicine (Asojo, Asuzu and Adebiyi, 2014). The involvement of the state government thus represents the localisation of the project half a century later, an institutional turn towards local engagement.

Strategic plans offer an incomplete, but nonetheless valuable, insight into how universities conceptualise their role in society. This analysis adds to our understanding of how a plan can uncover the tensions and complexities that organisations such as flagships are subject to. Whilst it is easy to overstate their importance or impact, strategies can – at least whilst they are current – have a live and ongoing role in steering decisions, however minor, in the face of changing circumstances. They can signify shifts and evolutions, acting as a 'probe into the future' (Albrechts, Balducci and Hillier, 2016, p. 15). The implications of these findings are now explored further.

CHAPTER 6

UNDERSTANDING THE MODERN FLAGSHIP UNIVERSITY

The previous chapters have sought to analyse the role of flagship universities in the development of sub-Saharan African city regions. This chapter attempts to draw everything together – not as a comprehensive summary, but to identify the main findings, presented under three broad headings. The first section looks at how flagships view their role in society and in their local area, and the factors that shape their positioning. The role of flagships is predominantly a national one, but to categorise them solely as such risks obscuring their important local and international functions. The second section examines local engagement activity more closely, and introduces a framework in which to consider funding barriers and institutional hurdles that need to be overcome before this activity is expanded. The final section brings together the traits of the modern flagship university, and the implications of these for their future.

How flagships conceptualise their role in society

The paths of African flagships are often entwined with their nations. The fortunes of the University of Ibadan closely followed that of Nigeria, with several distinct phases emerging for both since the 1960s. The University of Zimbabwe has had a fractious and polarised relationship with the state, witnessing proxy battles between government and opposition within university staff and students – the campus as the nation in microcosm. The birth and growth of an independent Namibian government mirrored that of its namesake university, drawing upon the same pool of people to fill their ranks. The National University of Rwanda was implicated in the 1994 genocide, and the University of Rwanda was formed as part of a strong, state-led vision of national development.

How do African flagship universities conceptualise their role in their local area through their strategic planning? It is first necessary to understand the extent of autonomy that these institutions are afforded, as this circumscribes and frames their role. Simultaneously influential yet vulnerable, most flagships are reliant on government funding, and are seeking to diversify their income (some, such as Makerere and the University of Ghana, are treating this as a top priority, recognising the risks of relying on government funding). Yet this transition is a slow process, and the path of marketisation is itself not without risks. Flagships are also often embedded within government-owned regulatory structures, staff are sometimes civil servants, and governments may have the power to appoint chancellors or vice chancellors. Professor Walter Kamba, University of Zimbabwe vice chancellor in the 1980s, summarised the implications of this in a 1995 paper which holds true today.

> *The development of the university is dependent on the support of those who work in it and on the availability of resources from the government. If the university accepts that university autonomy and academic freedom can only be perceived in the socio-economic context in which it operates, and that it depends on the goodwill of the nation and the sense of responsibility of the academic staff; if the government accepts that the university needs a certain amount of autonomy to carry out its mission effectively and efficiently, then there need not be a conflict between national aspirations and academic integrity. Any unbridled provincialism on the part of the university is as threatening to public and national interest, as is the desire of the state to police the university for the sake of control itself.*

> *Put differently, some state control is inescapable just as some substantial degree of institutional autonomy is indispensable. This is a balance which needs to be worked at, all the time. The task is to develop consultative relationships that bring the legitimate concerns of the university and the legitimate concerns of government into shared perspectives. (Kamba in Mohamedbhai, 2021)*

Flagships engage in a constant balancing act – a recurring theme of the past few chapters. There are tensions between fulfilling historic roles and meeting modern demands, prioritising traditional university functions and economic development efforts, putting self-interest or altruism first, and in the seemingly mundane framing of everyday interactions – when the university works with the community, are these people stakeholders or beneficiaries? Chapter 5 argued that flagships seek, through necessity, to find areas of alignment between their core mandate and opportunities to make money. This inevitably leads to a diffusion of activity, and a constant stream of trade-offs and compromises – a pattern not dissimilar to that found in university systems around the world.

The parameters of flagship activity are defined by their financial and political autonomy, and emerge as a product of this complex balancing act. They are part of society, but also a reflection of it. They serve society, but also provide a space for society. This is well-expressed by the 'instrumental' and 'intrinsic' pathways outlined in Chapter 2 (Unterhalter and Howell, 2021, p. 13). The university is a contributor of ideas, but also a forum for discussion and public debate. Some flagships have targets to increase their public engagement. At the University of Rwanda, contribution to public debate is regarded as either a strength, or an area in need of investment, depending on who one speaks to (Ransom, 2023, p. 172). Yet it has also been suggested that nearby hotels may be performing this role as an arena for meeting and discussion instead

(Ransom, 2023, p. 146), perhaps reflecting the neglect of public, collective spaces in many cities (Bekker, Croese and Pieterse, 2021, p. 2). Hotels are a very different form of anchor institution to a university, but they can also play a significant role in national and local development.

Conceptualising a local role

University strategic plans allow us insight into how flagships view their global, national and local roles – a manifestation of the interconnections and contradictions of the 'glonacal'. Some strategies attempt to make links between the scales, and especially between the local and global. The phrasing of these 'think global, act local'-type mantras is often devoid of concrete detail and risks becoming, in the words of Markusen (1999), a 'fuzzy concept': one that is malleable and nebulous, meaning different things to different people. Yet in both the literature and in practice, there is recognition that territories overlap and intersect, and that there is often no clear divide between different scales. The international, national and local are often messy and difficult to disentangle; a configuration of personal relationships, institutional histories and projects and programmes unique for each university and each city region. Internationalisation is sometimes viewed as a means of strengthening national development efforts, but the practice of bringing in international consultants can also undermine local capacity.

Nonetheless, the ten strategic plans – themselves a complex balancing act, and subject to government influence – presented a clear picture of how flagships view their position in society. A national role dominates, with well-developed plans to align activity to national frameworks reflecting the traditional role of the flagship university. The key to succeeding, according to the plans, will be to produce relevant research (the next few sections cover how feasible this is) and employable graduates. An international role features strongly too – although this is often framed in terms of loose aspirations to become a 'world-class university'; at the international level, the emphasis on contribution that defines the national role shifts to competition. A local role, including engagement with communities, is discussed in all plans, albeit to varying extents. Several recognise that the expectations of communities are not being met; local engagement is seen as an area that universities need to develop. Local and international roles are sufficiently elaborated to the extent that they would be alien to the developmental university of the 1970s, but they are nonetheless adjuncts to an unequivocal national focus.

These findings reinforce and build upon Marginson and Rhoades' (2002) glonacal agency heuristic, in particular by demonstrating that scales of place cannot be separated and need to be viewed as interrelated dimensions. To use the terminology of the heuristic, a modern flagship university is an agency working across local, national and global scales. It also *has* agency – although this is circumscribed by its close links with government, perhaps limiting its ability to 'construct the region' as theorised by Addie (2019a) with reference to European and North American universities. Other factors, again drawn from the heuristic, help describe the universities' local role (Marginson and Rhoades, 2002, pp. 291–293). 'Reciprocity', the two-way interactions of ideas and activity, is illustrated by the circulation of staff, as well as formal and informal pathways to engagement. 'Strength', the force and size of activity, is illustrated by the influence of government, the limited resource for local engagement activity, but also the few key individuals within universities who pioneer this activity. 'Layers and conditions' are the historic structures on which this activity is based, and the national development apparatus, the history of the university and the history of higher education in Africa all help to determine the scope and nature of activity. Finally, 'spheres of agency', the geographical extent of activity, are closely related to the distribution of campuses and the interpersonal relationships of staff members – for example between a lecturer and an official at city hall.

This book also seeks to add to our understanding of how strategic plans offer a window (albeit only ever a partial one) into institutional priorities. In Chapter 4, several previous papers were summarised, including an analysis of 78 strategies by Stensaker et al. (2019) which found a 'snakelike procession' of unranked universities aspiring towards medium-low ranked institutions, and medium-low ranked universities towards high-ranked ones. The strategies of African flagship universities are unlikely to sit neatly within the relatively homogenous three categories identified by Stensaker et al. Although most fit within the medium-low or unranked categories, and are resource-poor compared to most high-ranked universities, they have prominent national status. This means they simultaneously possess high prestige given their historic position at the centre of higher education in their country, and a set of pressures that compel them to look globally even though they may be unranked. Their aspirations to be world-class sit alongside both the pragmatism found in the unranked university strategies, and the focus on national development of the low-medium-ranked strategies. As both an actor in and a reflection of society, and with their complex and multifaceted roles, flagships escape easy categorisation.

How flagships conduct local engagement activity

The delicate balancing act of African flagships and the context these institutions operate within are shaped by the extent of autonomy they are afforded. These 'conditions of possibility' are historical and contemporary (Unterhalter and Howell, 2021, p. 13). As a result, flagships conceptualise their role primarily as institutions acting in service of the nation. This may suggest a highly curtailed local role, raising the question of to what extent and how do African flagship universities coordinate or participate in local engagement activity in their city regions.

The preceding chapters have provided examples of engagement across the ten universities. Some of this was viewed as local activity in plans; in other cases the examples were in pursuit of national objectives but largely took place within communities. This distinction between the location of work and the scale of objectives is further evidence of blurring, a two-way interaction, between the local and national scales. In Chapter 5 we saw how framings differ between universities: for some local activity was discussed in terms of service or engagement or outreach, for others the focus was on industry links and knowledge exchange. Some used the term Corporate Social Responsibility, others preferred talk of building community capacity. The literature on engagement is predominantly Northern and suggests that we have witnessed a broadening from 'third mission' activity as commercially-driven engagement to a plethora of economic, social and community-oriented activities (Tuunainen in Nelles and Vorley, 2010, p. 6). More work is needed to understand the typologies of engagement in African universities, but the analysis in this book suggests a similar breadth of activity amongst African flagships, although perhaps tracking more closely the priorities of the nation – whether that is the expansion of the private sector or meeting the needs of rural communities.

Community engagement has historic roots in African universities. For most flagships, local communities tend to be treated as a beneficiary rather than an equal partner in strategic planning for engagement activity. Bottom-up influence from the community is rare, and not encouraged or expected. Communities do not appear to be a stakeholder in university planning processes, nor do they appear to have strong influence on the university – 'counterextension', to use the terminology of de Sousa Santos (2010).

The conditions of possibility that form the parameters of flagship activity directly inform local engagement activity. Financial constraints and the drive to diversify income pushes one form of engagement – consultancy – above others, such as working alongside communities. Consultancy has been a recurring theme, from tensions with service at the birth of the developmental university model to being featured as a strategic objective. Employability is another theme that can be traced throughout the chapters, and it is interwoven with engagement: as pressures to produce employable graduates continue to increase, close links with business are privileged as a form of engagement – and again likely at the expense of other forms such as community-based programmes. Both diversification of income and a focus on the employability agenda are hallmarks of the sweeping marketisation of global higher education, although both also have echoes in the traditional developmental university model, where 'moonlighting' gave lecturers experience with industry (stoking fears of absenteeism from campus), and where skilled graduates were expected to drive the development of the nation.

The need for financial sustainability and employable graduates dominate the priorities of flagship universities. Areas deemed less critical nonetheless feature prominently in strategic plans: producing societally-relevant research is unanimous, and all discuss local and community engagement, with half having targets and implementation plans for increasing this. Given the weight of other priorities, how might these goals be realised? Or, in the framing of van Schalkwyk and de Lange (2018), can a form of university-community engagement that values place-specific development (and simultaneously strengthens teaching and research) exist in the face of such strong market logics?

A path to local engagement

There is a limited literature on the obstacles to increasing research in African universities, and some of this covers societally-relevant research with communities, including incentives for staff and institutional structures (Chapter 7). Kaweesi, Bisaso and Ezati (2019) and Ssembatya (2020), for example, give valuable insight into the processes and complexities around securing research funding. We can build on the analysis of the previous chapters to extend this work to local engagement, and model the path to starting a programme of local engagement activity at a flagship university.

Figure 3 provides an example of the decisions and circumstances that stand before a university starting a programme of local engagement work.[23] It provides a framework in which to consider funding barriers and institutional hurdles that need to be overcome. The decision tree is necessarily generalised and individual universities may skip all or part of the tree, or begin the process from a different starting point – that is, somewhere other than at the very top. In addition, whilst following the 'no' boxes in particular may result in questions that do not appear to logically connect, they aim to capture the main circumstances in which engagement work could begin by addressing each of the major incentives and barriers in turn. Answers to the questions in the clear boxes determine the path through the tree. The dark shaded box marks the start of a programme of local engagement activity; the light shaded boxes mark a failure to begin local activity, or the start of activity but in a limited form. Outcomes represent structured programmes; further work is needed to map pathways to unstructured interactions, informal engagement, and the intrinsic capacity of the university.

There are three key points. First, unless an institution can secure dedicated funding up front, the path to beginning a programme of work is both lengthy and complex, with numerous hurdles (this is also consistent with the literature on research funding in Chapter 7). Second, paths through the tree may differ for a large university in West Africa compared to a similarly-sized counterpart in, for example, South East England. The former will typically have to go through many more steps as dedicated funding for local engagement activity can be lacking; in the UK such funding is relatively plentiful – universities have accessed decades worth of European Structural and Investment Funding, UK government infrastructure and local growth funds in various guises, and small but flexible pots of money such as the Higher Education Innovation Fund – although barriers do exist.[24] The availability of skilled staff to administer and deliver local engagement programmes could be seen as a further differentiating factor, but this is likely a function of having had consistent funding for this purpose in the past. Third, an effective and sustainable programme requires institutional support, staff or student willingness, and appropriate resources. Eschewing any one of these three elements hinders local engagement. We have seen numerous examples of barriers in practice: vague policies, bureaucracy, ad-hoc support mechanisms, misaligned promotion criteria, high workloads and limited budgets.

---

23 This decision tree has been influenced by the academic literature, as well as the analysis in this book. It is also informed by my own professional experience of local engagement in UK higher education, and I have received helpful feedback from colleagues in both the UK and Rwanda. As before, local university engagement is defined here as projects, programmes, activities and relationships with external parties outside of the university, at a sub-national level. This may include research, innovation and community-focused projects, and social, cultural, environmental and economic programmes of work. Activities may be led by staff or students, or by an external partner with university support.

24 As with African universities, appropriate university structures and staff incentives are vitally important (Sánchez-Barrioluengo and Benneworth, 2019, p. 3). Even with these in place, the processes for accessing and spending, for example, European Structural and Investment Funds have sometimes been cumbersome, complex and somewhat trying for the staff involved (Giordano, 2020, p. 6). This particular funding stream has now ended following the UK's withdrawal from the European Union.

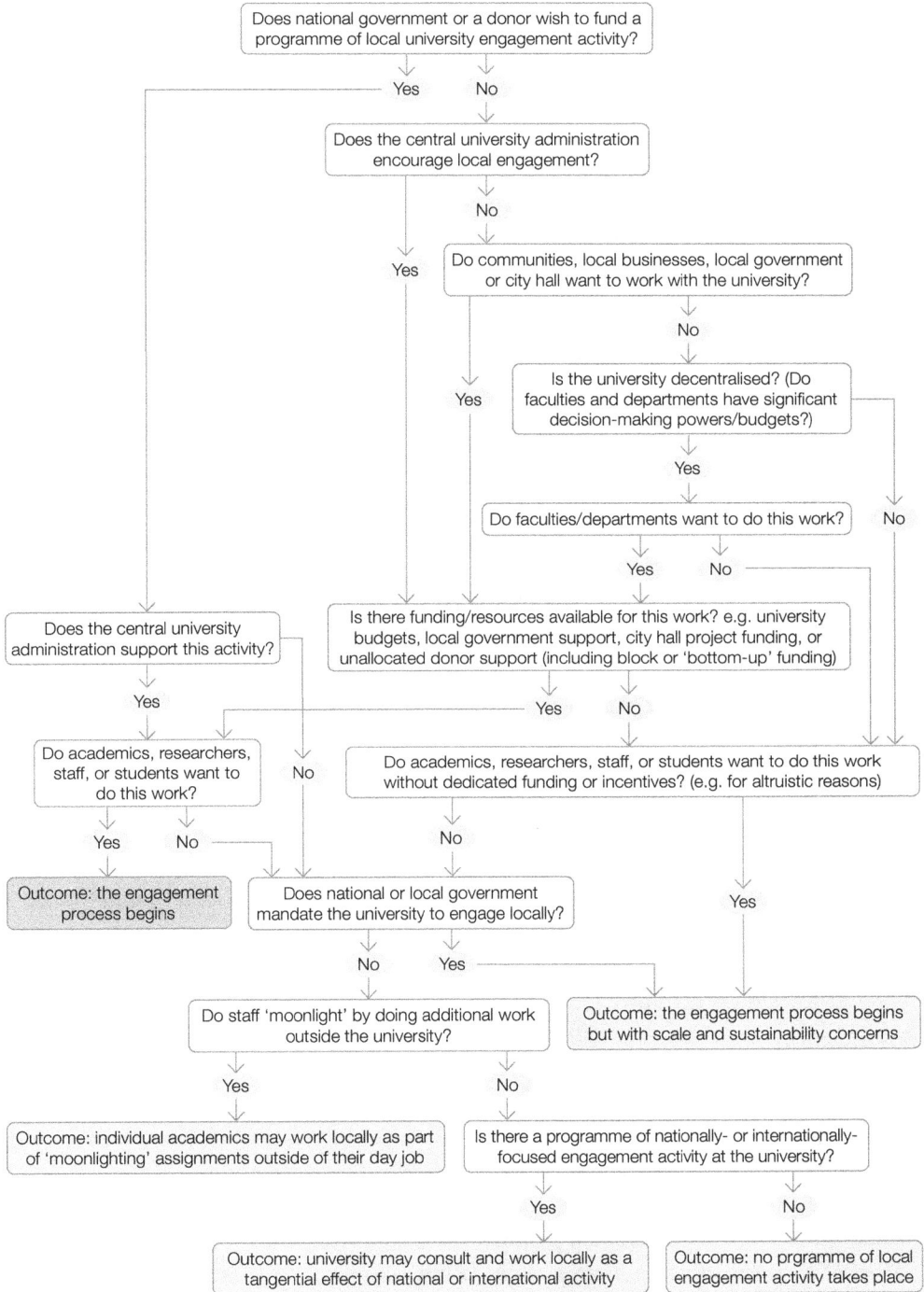

Figure 3 A decision tree showing the path to starting a local engagement programme

Of course, the story does not end once a programme of engagement begins. What makes for a successful local engagement programme – and who benefits – is another topic in need of substantial analysis within the African context. Although local engagement is subject to (somewhat rudimentary) key performance indicators in half of the ten flagships, and there are often strong monitoring frameworks that 'cascade' through the entire institution, the systems to track and evaluate engagement activity more broadly are lacking. There is also the need to reflect further upon what a successful outcome might look like. This could be the conceptualisation of the engaged civic university as developed by Goddard (2009, p. 5) – one which 'engages as a whole with its surroundings, not piecemeal'. Or it could be the call of van Schalkwyk and de Lange (2018, p. 1) for a shift from a form of community engagement driven by financial incentives to one that emphasises place-specific development, recognising that the fortunes of a university are often closely intertwined with the health of its locality. The likelihood of these shifts taking place is wrapped up in notions of the 'ideal' university, and we have seen how these evolve over time. It will also depend upon, and be shaped by, the traits of the flagship university.

How the characteristics of flagships shape local engagement activity

If the University of Rwanda moved its Kigali campuses 380 kilometres to Kampala, or 1,500 kilometres to Lusaka, would it broadly function the same? Would a University of Ibadan in Accra, or a University of Namibia in Addis Ababa, face the same challenges and have the same impact? This book has maintained that the ten African flagships examined, whilst rooted in their individual places and histories, nonetheless share a set of traits and characteristics that define their role in society. Whether formed in 1918 or 2013, they carry the inheritance of the developmental university model, and they have been shaped by the same forces transforming higher education across the continent and the world. They have more in common than separates them. Whilst this does not mean that a policy prescription for one can be blindly applied to all, it does mean that discussions about the transformative potential of flagships, and debates over their future role, are broadly relevant. This section asks what are the traits of African flagship universities, and how do these shape local engagement activity?

Some traits directly impact local engagement, and the form it takes. We have explored consultancy in considerable detail, how it is a product of the mechanics of work for university staff, and how it leads to a certain form of knowledge transfer driven by external demand. Staff at flagships are also often in demand as experts to serve on boards and committees, and to act as policy commentators. Flagship universities deliver public services, including public health outreach, support to farmers, and legal advice clinics.

Other traits indirectly impact local engagement. Flagships are often 'mother institutions' – mentors to other higher education institutions, a little-recognised hallmark of the flagship university but one with long-term implications for engagement. University models are often cloned when sibling institutions are born, and these can be hard to later change. Mentorship is a noble sacrifice: not only does setting up new universities demand the time of flagship university staff, but the fledgling institutions then compete for government funds, students, and staff (who may be paid better than at the flagship). Importantly, mentorship often also marks a geographic spread of higher education provision outside the capital, with implications for the centrality and connectivity of city regions. Flagships themselves have mirrored this process, with the universities of Ghana, Makerere, Namibia, Rwanda and Zambia in particular having multiple campuses and extensive physical footprints, sometimes extending outside their capitals (for Ghana and Makerere especially this has been driven by the imperative of institutional decentralisation). A final trait worthy of mention here, significant for its pervasiveness in Africa, is the circulation of staff between universities, government and parastatals – there is often a constellation of offices that senior personnel move around. Interfaces between the flagship university and government are often well-developed; the university is deeply intertwined in networks and is part of a broad government apparatus of institutions aimed at driving development. The impression given is not of cross-sector collaboration and helping institutions to work coherently together, but *service* more broadly to the nation: how can this person best meet national development needs? This seeping impact into government, city halls and the machinery of national development extends to that of alumni – exemplified by the two-thirds of senior Zambian officials and MPs who graduated from their national flagship. Flagships have an indelible influence on the decision makers who shape society.

In Chapter 5 these traits were split into two groups: one that speaks to the influence of the marketisation and corporatisation of higher education, and another that pulls away from this, asserting the unique public role of the flagship as embodied in its founding role. The signature trait of the flagship university is to manage the tension between these two groups, to reconcile them in the name of national relevance and to ensure institutional survival. In the day-to-day turmoil of budget crises, leadership changes and political upheaval, this tension can appear to be slipping, with the university on the verge of collapse (for example, the insolvency of the University of Zambia). Yet there has been talk of flagships fighting for survival since at least the 1980s (both Coleman (1986) and Court (1980) touch on this), and flagships have proved resilient: battered, no doubt, by resource constraints, government interference, the imposition of market reforms, restructures and decentralisation and strikes and protests, but continuing nonetheless to survive and evolve.[25] As such, a benefit of Chapter 3 has been to put the traits of flagships into historical perspective. The Scottish roots of the University of Cape Town, the role of the University of London in the formation of the universities of Ibadan, Zimbabwe and others, and the eclectic influences on Addis Ababa University all had lasting impact. Problems that are pressing today have often been pressing for decades – funding for research at the University of Ghana has been an issue since at least the 1970s (Dickson, 1973, p. 113), and the readiness of graduates for work was a concern in the 1960s.

---

25 This tendency to foresee the demise of the university may be universal. Frank and Meyer (2007, p. 291) observe that there is a long history of observers predicting the collapse of higher education institutions as we know them: 'the university over the last several decades has enjoyed stunning success ... but the literature is curiously wary in tone'. Universities have thrived, the authors contend, because they help drive integration into global society. This institutional isomorphism is revisited in Chapter 7.

This is not to suggest that change is impossible, but that meaningful change will require more than simple policy prescriptions. Path dependency is a real phenomenon at African flagships. When an academic centre is founded and funded by a donor, it can set in motion decades of research in a particular field, setting generations of researchers and students on a particular path. If this path is misaligned with national or local priorities, the opportunity cost for the university, for communities and the nation can be huge (Ssembatya, 2020, p. 13). Brain drain and staff shortages mean pipelines of academic talent cannot develop, the effects of which compound over time; there is good reason why philanthropic organisations such as the Carnegie Foundation focus on academic workforce development (Acquah and Budu, 2017, p. 150).

It is striking that, with one exception, the ten universities in this study do not describe themselves as flagships, but prefer to describe themselves in terms of aspirations: to be a research university, or a world-class university. Does this render Teferra's definition of a flagship (from Chapter 2) obsolete? From the analysis in this book, the definition still holds strong, as it recognises the unique influence and history of these institutions. Teferra (2016, p. 82) also acknowledges the isomorphism that is perhaps driving this push for a greater research role. Governments have also encouraged this push, with authorities in Ghana (Cloete, Bunting and van Schalkwyk, 2018, p. 241) and Ethiopia (Tamrat, 2020) establishing tiered university systems in recent years, and their respective flagships working hard to meet the (top) classification of a research university in response.

Research is not the only path to increasing local engagement activity in the future, but it is a significant one. Aligning research and local engagement can help to meet the demand for relevance. Kaweesi, Bisaso and Ezati (2019, p. 14) interviewed academics at Makerere and found the majority viewed socially relevant research as the 'ultimate measure of a research-led flagship university'. Although most flagships lead in measurements of research output and publications in their country, they struggle to fund and maintain this activity, especially in the face of high numbers of undergraduates. As a result, donors who fund research have an outsized influence; the recommendations in Chapter 7 present some initial ideas on channelling this support to meet local needs. Before then, some final thoughts on the role of African flagship universities in the development of city regions are offered.

Is there evidence of a local turn?

Community engagement was exhorted as a priority at the founding of the University of Rwanda in 2013, it is a pillar of the strategic plan today, and it is a common theme in the speeches of vice chancellors and ministers of education. This book sought to ask: is local engagement happening in practice? More broadly, are flagship universities in African city regions developing a local focus alongside their historic national mission?

There is a local dimension to the activity of flagship universities, demonstrated by the ten cases in this study. However, academics have distinguished between the university that sees itself as simply *in* the city versus the university as *part of* or *for* the city (Goddard, Kempton and

Vallance, 2013, p. 43), or between universities in urban areas versus urban universities (Addie, 2016, p. 4). The former happen to be located in a place, whereas the latter see their place as central to their identity and mission. African flagships may be *in* city regions, but they are not *for* those city regions. They are unmistakably for their nation; they are usually *the* public university. However, city regions are places where the international coexists with the local, and the centre is entangled with the periphery. Local engagement is a viable and visible means of contributing to national development, and it offers the potential to enhance student teaching and complement staff research. As we saw with the multiversity model in Chapter 2, the local is a further 'accretion' in the ever-expanding remit of the flagship university, a multipurpose institution at arms length from government (although the length of the arm differs) that can be tasked with solving ever more issues.

There is also a simpler framing: like the oft-quoted phrase about politics, ultimately the implementation of all development projects is local. And so, as the focus on the development role of flagship universities has increased – through the accretion of roles and responsibilities, but also through agendas such as the Sustainable Development Goals and Agenda 2063 – so too has implementation activity, and a local turn has taken place.

There are, of course, exceptions to the notion that all development projects are local. Although much outreach, consultancy and research activity is rooted in a physical location, some forms of engagement are not directly delivered in a place. Providing evidence for government policymaking, for example, can remain resolutely national in focus. Yet even here universities can play a role in terms of introducing a place lens: how do proposed policies play out across different places? Are the benefits and risks evenly spread? Should decisions be devolved to city or regional level, and what role can evidence play in strengthening this process?

Despite growing attention on the role of higher education in development, there has been limited analysis of how universities engage with and contribute to the development of their local surroundings, particularly in sub-Saharan Africa. This book has sought to address this gap. In doing so, it has revealed that there is much in common between flagship universities in Africa, and the challenges and opportunities they face, despite their individual histories. However, the role of universities in society and in their local area has a resonance beyond the continent. Kamola (2014) captures the duality between the personal path of an institution, and its inescapable participation in global higher education systems.

> *African universities remind us that all universities are primarily political institutions with their own complicated and particular histories. Today, African universities cannot be understood independent of their colonial legacy, their struggles for national liberation, or the decades of economic crises that followed. In short, African universities – like all universities – are not singular and isolated institutions but rather multiple, complex, and contradictory sites of world politics. (Kamola, 2014, p. 604)*

The concluding chapter briefly considers this bigger picture.

CHAPTER 7

FINAL THOUGHTS AND FUTURE CONSIDERATIONS

This book has told the story of the roles that ten flagship universities play in their societies. Although the details are rooted in African city regions, the question this research aimed to answer is a much broader one: what role does a university play in its local area? Along the way, this book has sought to provide insight into the traits of the modern flagship university, and how these are similar to and differ from the developmental university model. It helps us to better understand practices of local engagement and how these intersect with broader institutional priorities and national development agendas. It also bridges several academic disciplines where interaction has been limited but the potential for mutual learning is significant: higher education and development studies on one hand, and regional and urban studies on the other. More broadly, it contributes to the literature on African higher education, on the role of universities in development, and the relationship between universities and place.

This final chapter takes a step back, first by positioning these debates within the field of research on university engagement in Africa and the divides and commonalities between the Global North and South; and then by looking at the significance of the topic for universities and governments, first by briefly examining the trend towards isomorphism in higher education, and then suggesting some areas for future work.

Revisiting university engagement in Africa

Literature on engagement in Africa often has a single-country focus, and in many cases employs a single university as case study. Mtawa and Wangenge-Ouma (2021) examined the motivations for university-community engagement within a public university in Tanzania, and found that this activity is often treated as an 'add-on' to advance the interests of academics. They call for better institutional support to drive genuine engagement with communities. Mupeta et al. (2020) studied 'civic entrepreneurship' – projects undertaken for the greater good of society with no expectation of financial benefit – at the University of Zambia. Although this contribution is an institutional priority, they find that there are numerous challenges in implementation: political interference in the governance of the university, bureaucracy, inefficient communication processes across and within departments, and a lack of money. Also in Zambia, Zulu et al. (2019) reflect on a community engagement project which failed to secure the consent of most participants, and share the importance of building trust and understanding local values. Onwuemele (2018) looked at community engagement at several Nigerian universities, and concludes that incentives and promotion structures fail to reward work that benefits local communities. Kaweesi, Bisaso and Ezati (2019) and Ssembatya (2020) both examine the processes and complexities around securing research funding to meet local needs, and both use Makerere University in Uganda as a case study. They call for more balanced partnerships with donors and other institutions, and improved appointment and promotion policies for university staff. There is a more developed literature on engagement in South Africa. In *Anchored in Place: Rethinking the university and development in South Africa*, Bank, Cloete and van Schalkwyk (2018) present case studies of city-campus relationships at several universities. The book seeks to promote a greater role for universities as agents of place-based growth and socio-cultural change, noting the role some universities play in this regard in Europe and North America (Bank, Cloete and van Schalkwyk, 2018, p. 6). Other notable examples from South Africa include a highly-developed understanding of partnership dynamics between the University of KwaZulu-Natal and the local community set out by Mutero (2021), and an assessment of Nelson Mandela Metropolitan University's (NMMU) engagement with place by van Schalkwyk and de Lange (2018). The authors find that despite a strong place-based focus, engagement at NMMU is largely opportunistic rather than motivated by the problems faced by the city's communities.

Several studies extend beyond national borders. The work of Bekele and colleagues has cast a wider look at university-society partnerships in Africa, including through analysis of strategic plans and the development of methodological frameworks (Bekele and Ofoyuru, 2021; Bekele, Cossa and Barat, 2021; Bekele, Ofoyuru and Woldegiorgis, 2024). In a study of university engagement with communities in secondary cities (primarily in South Africa, but also in Cameroon and Kenya), Fongwa et al. (2022) find practices of engagement have roots in the founding principles of African universities as well as traditional societal values, although the emphasis on benefits for broader society have been tempered by globalisation and neoliberal pressures. Analysis of community engagement through service learning by Mtawa (2019) is again rooted in South Africa, but is written with a view to wider debates in sub-Saharan Africa and the Global South. Service learning is an approach whereby 'staff and students and external communities establish sustainable partnerships and participate in activities that empower them' (Mtawa, 2019, p. 9). Rather than a panacea for deep-rooted societal challenges, service learning is presented as a means for promoting human development and the common good. Finally, an edited volume by Watson et al. (2011) presents case studies from members of the Talloires Network of Engaged Universities, with contributions from multiple continents, including African representation from South Africa, Sudan and Tanzania. This examination of civic engagement foretells one of the common challenges from the studies above, published more recently: that appropriate incentives and reward structures are vital for sustaining this activity. The study also concludes that departments and institutions with less prestige are often more pioneering in their engagement activity (Watson et al., 2011, p. xxviii). That the editors found so many issues in common across universities in the North and South, and that institutions in the South have a greater emphasis on improving community conditions and do so with smaller budgets, suggests there may be a valuable transferability of the learning from African flagships in this book to counterparts elsewhere.[26]

Occasionally one also encounters isolated examples of local university engagement elsewhere, such as the literature on urban development. Addis Ababa University has established a Railway Engineering Institute to train engineers to maintain the city's new light rail transit; all students are employed by the Ethiopian Railway Corporation (Kassahun, 2021, p. 166). In Kisumu, Kenya, the two local universities have partnered with the city and county administrations, civil society and the chamber of commerce to form the Kisumu Local Interaction Platform, and have addressed urban planning problems in the city, including the redevelopment of marketplaces (Smit, 2018, p. 71). Caution should, however, be extended to these examples. Whilst they may provide an insight into what is possible, they may not be representative (perhaps having been selected for their novelty), and the notion of 'best practice' is problematic. Pike, Rodríguez-Pose and Tomaney (2007, p. 1263) observe that whilst questions such as 'what works?' and 'what are the successful models?' appear to be neutral, they cannot be considered within a vacuum, outside politics. They add that the search for pragmatic, short-term solutions can limit difficult but sustainable public policy responses to local and regional development challenges.

Divides and commonalities between North and South

Much of the literature on local engagement and the role of universities in society – including that cited in previous chapters – originates from, and is concerned with, the Global North. Whilst often recognising that a simplistic split between North and South masks a great deal of variation within each, academics in the South have called for the contextualisation of theories and concepts imported from the North, and to strengthen the production of work grounded in the South (sub-Saharan African examples include Bank, Cloete and van Schalkwyk, 2018, p. 7; Mtawa, 2019, p. 6; Fongwa et al., 2022, p. 3).

There are two further observations regarding the relationship between North and South that relate specifically to the generation of knowledge on local university engagement, and therefore are relevant to the discussions in this book. First, cities across the North and South are seen as important actors in coordinating responses to global challenges, and are active participants in networks and other fora that cross continents (Acuto, 2016, p. 612). This partly reflects that a city dweller in Durban, South Africa may have more in common with a resident of Dundee, Scotland than with their fellow citizens in a village 50 kilometres away. It also underscores the interconnected nature of global challenges, illustrated by COVID-19, but perhaps more accurately demonstrated by climate change. What happens in one place has repercussions elsewhere, with little distinction

---

26 It should be noted that the universities featured in Watson et al. (2011) self-identify as 'engaged'. As of September 2024, the Talloires Network of Engaged Universities has 437 signatory member institutions in 86 countries (Talloires Network, 2024). Of these, the University of Cape Town, the University of Ghana, Makerere University, the University of Rwanda and the University of Zimbabwe are featured in this book.

between North and South, and no acknowledgement of national borders. The result, as called for by Oldekop et al. (2020), is a need for 'global' rather than 'international' development, for recognition that the North does not have all the expertise to tackle global challenges, for multi-directional learning, and for a focus on all countries and places rather than nation states in the North 'helping' those in the South. As such, the contribution of flagship universities in city regions in Africa to the Sustainable Development Goals (SDGs), for example, is of relevance to multi-faculty institutions in the UK and elsewhere.

Second, although the literature on universities and development and the literature on universities and place are mostly separate, there has been some recent mutual interaction between the broader fields of local and regional development (historically focused on Europe and North America), and the international development literature (largely concerned with low-income countries). These two large, multidisciplinary fields have in the past operated on separate tracks from one another (Pike, Rodríguez-Pose and Tomaney, 2017, p. 48), but as inequality has become a deep concern, globalisation has been critiqued, and the implication of interdependence between nations is increasingly apparent, the overlap is being explored. Underpinning this is a recognition that there is no one 'correct' development path, and mutual learning is needed. On one side, MacKinnon et al. (2021, p. 11) suggest policymakers focused on local and regional development consider a broader view of development beyond measures of GDP, productivity and growth to include livelihoods, wellbeing and social infrastructure (such as community services, housing and belonging). This so-called endogenous development is inspired in part by research in development studies. In addition, the concept of 'inclusive innovation' has become prevalent in public policy and particularly as part of urban planning. It has its roots in the field of international development (Lee, 2020). So too does inclusive growth, a 'new mantra' for local economic policymaking (Lee, 2019, p. 432). On the other side, notions such as 'decentralised development co-operation' reflect a reinvigorated appreciation of the importance of sub-national governance and local processes for development and for the SDGs (Moreira da Silva and Kamal-Chaoui, 2019) – mirrored in widespread devolution unfolding across much of Africa (Iddawela, Lee and Rodríguez-Pose, 2021, p. 3). Work on 'translocal development' bridges local and international development by emphasising the flow of people, capital and ideas (Westen et al., 2021). This book has aimed to provide a similar point of intersection between these fields with higher education at the centre.

Institutional isomorphism and broader relevance

A reader familiar with university systems in the Global North may be struck by the similarities to issues faced by the African flagship universities in this study. Vice chancellors in Addis Ababa and Aberdeen both need to contend with how best to demonstrate a commitment to employability and to 'relevance', to weigh up the merits of institutional decentralisation or whether to expand or shrink the courses on offer, and how the next five- or ten-year strategic plan can bind the university together and keep stakeholders happy. In this study, isomorphism manifests as African flagships seeking to become world-class universities, and attempting to emulate research universities within the upper echelons of global league tables. This represents a divergence from peers in their countries (who, in general, seek regional or national prestige), yet they are unavoidably and irrevocably rooted, through history and through their developmental role, in their nations. As a result, the African flagship, by definition, is quite dissimilar to both a research intensive university in, say, the UK and a private, vocational institution in, for example, Uganda. In their country, flagships stand apart but are also deeply linked; collectively across the continent they share a rich set of traits and challenges. Flagships are expected to be both a vehicle for national (and increasingly local) transformation, and globally competitive; they are an embodiment of the inseparable scales of place, but also the tensions between them.

Academic debates on institutional isomorphism and the internationalisation of higher education intersect neatly onto the contours of this study of African flagships. Over thirty years ago, Levinson (1989, p. 23) lamented a shift taking place in US universities towards homogenous bureaucracies and a 'growing abundance of managers and officials on campus'. Over the following decades the functions of the university have continued to increase, with 'a wave of managerialism' washing over universities globally, representing a 'rapid proliferation of linkages between the university and the wider society' (Frank and Meyer, 2007, p. 290).

This pattern has been mirrored in higher education systems across the world, and there have been numerous attempts to capture this interplay between the international and the local. We have explored the glonacal framework of Marginson and Rhoades (2002), which emphasised the importance of looking beyond national policy and attempting to understand global forces and local patterns. Vaira (2004, p. 485) introduced the concept of 'organisational allomorphism' to explain how globalisation leads to homogenisation and convergence in institutional structures, but that these have local variations shaped by local contexts. Frank and Meyer (2007, p. 289) conclude that 'in the university, in short, the local particularities both of that which is known and those who know are increasingly reconstituted in global and universal terms'. As the creation of a globally competitive knowledge society has become the ideal of national policymakers, the modern research university – which African flagships aspire to – has emerged as the most important actor in these efforts (Powell, Baker and Fernandez, 2017; Zapp and Ramirez, 2019, p. 5).

However, this study also offers insights for those looking at higher education beyond the African continent. The ten flagships offer a case study of large universities tasked with supporting national development but needing to reconcile local and international roles, operating in resource-poor environments, and balancing often complex relationships with national governments. They can also tell us about community engagement in low- and middle-income settings, and conceptualisations and framings of place. As such, this study can help build on studies in diverse locations: from flagship universities in Kazakhstan (Kuzhabekova, Soltanbekova and Almukhambetova, 2018; Gafu, 2019) to community universities in southern Brazil (Fioreze and McCowan, 2018).

Whilst the research university may be flourishing as an institutional model, the processes of isomorphism and internationalisation have been far from universally welcomed. We have seen criticism of marketisation and neoliberal policies, and the withering effects these can have on academics (for example Felde et al.). Convergence can hide power imbalances, in particular between institutions in the North and South (Kraemer-Mbula et al., 2019; Asare, Mitchell and Rose, 2020). The conformity and lack of originality of the research university model has been critiqued, including by former leaders of such institutions (Thrift, 2022). Nor are the local and the global always as neatly reconciled as theories suggest. Teferra (2020, p. 160) argues that widely adopted definitions of internationalisation, which emphasise intentionality and agency, are unsuited to the South as institutions there are coerced into playing the internationalisation game on the terms of the North – a similar charge to that levelled at strategic plans in Chapter 4 (this charge does, however, mask the wide diversity in university systems and forms of internationalisation in the South). As such, institutions 'vigorously pursue aspects of internationalisation under duress'. He argues that internationalisation needs to be more rooted in local contexts and needs.

Although planners and officials may uphold the modern research university as an institutional 'ideal', the entrepreneurial university model has also influenced African flagships. However, there are multiple interpretations within the academic literature of what an entrepreneurial university is. Cerver Romero, Ferreira and Fernandes (2020) describe these as different 'faces' of the entrepreneurial university, one of which promotes internationalisation and seeking new opportunities through global connections (demonstrating considerable overlap with the research university). Another 'face' is regional (that is, sub-national) and national development, and a more active role in the local environment. Sánchez-Barrioluengo and Benneworth (2019, p. 9) find that university entrepreneurial engagement converges around two models: a focus on specific knowledge transfer outcomes (usually with firms), or towards general contributions to regional economic development activity. These activities also permeate the strategic plans of lower ranked and unranked institutions – both in the study of plans by Stensaker et al. (2019), and in this book.

If we assume the tendency towards isomorphism of universities continues, what are the implications for African flagships? How will relevance be defined? Will flagships continue to 'accrete' new functions? Will the different faces of the entrepreneurial university become more pronounced, emphasising both global connectivity and local development? If the local grows in importance, will we see partnerships between city halls and flagship universities to, for example, attract foreign direct investment, as we have seen in Europe? Or – to borrow the terminology of Vaira (2004) – will a particular African declension, or local variation, emerge?

A study of a subject of this magnitude and complexity can only ever give us a partial picture, and one that is unavoidably from a particular vantage point and moment in time. With these limitations in mind, there are numerous areas both for future academic inquiry and for policymakers to consider.

Future considerations

There are three broad areas worthy of further work. The first is to extend thinking on the interface between research and community engagement, given how central research is within the plans of many flagship universities, and how it opens a potential stream of funding for local engagement activity. As domestic research funds are often limited, donors have outsized influence. Ssembatya (2020, p. 16) calls for less stringent funding restrictions, and recognises that some development partners have relaxed requirements, allowing funds to be used for supporting the research agenda of the university and for boosting institutional capacity building. Funders such as SIDA appear to encourage a more bottom-up approach. Often, however, this is not the case, as an academic at Makerere observes:

> *When donors come here, they have already decided on what they want. They are interested in people who think like them. Professors that work with them are not bringing their innovations [to] the work, but are just fitting into the donors' research agenda. If you are working with donor funds, you are working within the project funders' objectives. (Makerere academic quoted in Kaweesi, Bisaso and Ezati, 2019, p. 16)*

In this instance, external funding serves to promote the coercive elements of isomorphism, creating research centres in the donor's image. Who defines 'relevance' is of critical importance (Woldegiyorgis, Tamrat and Teferra, 2022). However, as demand grows for research to have practical outcomes and to inform policy, the potential for universities to incorporate community engagement into projects also increases – especially if they can make the case that local engagement complements national development priorities. Where engagement does take place, effort is needed to make it equitable and effective. Working *for* a community is a different proposition to working *alongside* a community. This is a subtle but important distinction, and separates efforts to work with communities from the very start (for example, in formulating research objectives) as part of a bottom-up effort, from superficial attempts to consult or involve community members. In other words, *engaging with a community as part of a project* is not necessarily the same as a *community engagement project*. A donor may say, 'see what the community thinks', but this is often not the same as seeking to discover what people in the community want from the university. Petersen, Kruss and van Rheede (2022, p. 890) encourage universities to take this a step further, and seek to co-produce not only scholarly outputs but development outcomes with communities.

A positive example of engagement is provided by Mutero et al. (2021, p. 131), who describe a public health project conducted by the University of KwaZulu-Natal. The team took personality tests to understand themselves and improve how they interact with the community. A Community Advisory Board acted as an entry-point into the community, explaining the research aims and objectives to the community, and communicating the expectations of the community to researchers. Research agendas were co-set together with community research assistants. Over time, community members have been trained in interviewing and data collection. The authors conclude that these processes 'demystify science as the preserve of the academy'.[27]

A couple of related developments are also worthy of more research. There is a trend towards prioritising interdisciplinary research in flagships, echoing the debates from the formation of the developmental university model. The University of Rwanda (2018b, p. 8) plan commits the university to developing 'interdisciplinary, problem-based academic programmes aligned with Rwanda's development needs'. Makerere University (2020, p. 11) plans to move towards larger, multidisciplinary, multi-institution research initiatives to promote national development. The University of Cape Town sees interdisciplinary research as a means to understand the past, and to define and tackle future problems (UCT, 2021b, p. 10). The University of Mauritius (2015, p. 7) strategic plan promotes the importance of 'innovative and interdisciplinary exploration'. The University of Ibadan's vice chancellor promised new interdisciplinary institutes, and added that 'I have always been a strong believer that some of the most exciting things in science and discoveries are at the boundary between different disciplines' (Olayinka, 2015, p. 20). Despite this wave of enthusiasm, there is little detail on how disciplines will work together in practice, and what the implications of this are for local engagement, especially at universities with several campuses and where there is often a degree of specialisation at each.

A further development is an increase in attempts to understand, protect and share indigenous knowledge – with some evidence of this in strategic plans. The Multidisciplinary Research Centre at the University of Namibia looks to collect and study indigenous knowledge; there are three nodes of the African Institute of Indigenous Knowledge Systems (AIIKS) at the University of Rwanda (Mbonyinshuti, 2021a); and Mbah, Johnson and Chipindi (2021) found that academics at the University of Zambia are becoming more deliberate in their engagement with indigenous knowledge, linking community engagement with sustainable development. Flagships are well-positioned to lead these efforts, and in doing so strengthen their engagement with communities.

The second broad area relates to the practices of engagement explored in this study. Grek (2021, p. 41) asserts that the education elites of today are often policy actors: 'people who occupy multiple spaces and who are simultaneously national and transnational, experts and brokers'. Given the expanding roles and accretions of the flagship university, it is unsurprising perhaps that the most influential individuals are often those who can move easily amongst different circles – manifesting, in this research, as staff circulation between the university, government and parastatals. Yet there is a parallel phenomenon of 'boundary spanners', covered predominantly by studies in the Global North.[28] Boundary spanners are individuals who work in one institution (such as a

---

27 We must also learn from examples of where communities refused to engage. For example, Zulu et al. (2019) met resistance from local communities when conducting a pilot project on school-based pregnancy prevention in rural Zambia. Although the research team (based at the University of Zambia and the University of Bergen, Norway) had ethical approval and permission from national and local officials, the majority of guardians refused to participate. In the UK, Melhuish (2015, p. 7) has described UCL's campus expansion into a difficult-to-access, historically deprived East London Olympic Park site (now an innovation district), and the difficulty of intervening in the fabric of communities in a sensitive manner that can engender a long-term relationship.

28 An exception sometimes witnessed outside of the North is the use of 'professors of practice', helping to bridge university and industry (Etzkowitz and Dzisah, 2008, p. 662).

university), but proactively work across sectors, building relationships and programmes of work. In some cases these may be joint appointments funded by two organisations, or a secondment. The field of boundary spanning leadership advocates cross-sector collaboration to find collective solutions to complex problems, with higher education leaders at the fore (Prysor and Henley, 2018), but boundary spanning has also been studied beyond senior leadership teams, for example, amongst staff in university business engagement roles (Martin and Ibbotson, 2019). Boundary spanning efforts often emphasise connections between different disciplines and policy domains, and have a focus on tackling local challenges, and therefore large universities tend to have a leading role, as do other anchor institutions such as hospitals (Stubbs, Dickson and Husbands, 2020; British Academy, 2021, p. 20; Chaytor, Gottlieb and Reid, 2021, p. 60). Further work could explore how staff circulation and boundary spanners reflect the higher education systems and societies in which they operate, and the potential for mutual learning and applicability in resource-poor environments.

There are practical steps that could support local activity at flagship universities. These include annual awareness workshops aimed at, for example, city hall staff (especially mid-level managers who have responsibility for transmitting information throughout the organisation, but are more involved in policy detail than the upper leadership team) to share relevant research topics. Consolidating published papers, staff details and summaries of policy or consulting work relating to local challenges into a single portal would allow easy access to university expertise – no simple task, but one that could facilitate greater uptake of knowledge outside of the university (at the University of Rwanda, for example, open access journals are fragmented and can be difficult to navigate) and raise awareness of the capabilities of the university. Funders supporting university research could offer technical assistance funding to bring in external partners at the start of projects to raise awareness and build relationships, whilst also building capacity within universities to work effectively with government and other partners. A larger undertaking is to build systems to track alumni. The University of Namibia, one of the newest flagships in this study, has over 17,000 graduates but no details of their subsequent careers. UNESCO notes that collecting this information would help improve the labour market relevance of the curriculum, and that alumni are a force to be harnessed for institutional development (presumably for fundraising), forging new partnerships, and assessing the impact of university education locally and further afield (UNESCO, 2016, p. 76).

Other trends may shape local activity in the future. Worldwide league table rankings have a pervasive impact on institutional decisions and national policies (Hazelkorn, 2007), and the focus on becoming recognised as 'world-class' suggests flagships are not immune from their influence. More recent rankings, such as the *Times Higher Education Impact Rankings*, aim to capture contributions to the Sustainable Development Goals, including through outreach activity (Lim, 2018, p. 423). However, staff at flagships may wish to also keep an eye on the proliferation of local economic impact studies commissioned by universities in the North (Guest and Ransom, 2020). This is an 'arms race' in a different form, swapping the quest for a higher global ranking for a bigger monetary contribution to the local economy. Notwithstanding the flaws inherent in many of these studies (Siegfried, Sanderson and McHenry, 2007), they are also laden with the perils of the 'impact' agenda, including short-termism and the erosion of open-ended academic inquiry (McCowan, 2018), and the shortcomings associated with the 'metric society' – a myopic focus on what can be measured above all else (Mau, 2019).

The final area represents a call for more work on the topics covered in this book, in particular the local role of universities in the Global South. This may involve studies in city regions on other continents, but also small and private institutions in Africa, universities in smaller towns and rural areas, and flagships in Francophone and Lusophone nations. A few other suggestions for further inquiry have been made in earlier chapters: how can we better understand the informal and intrinsic roles of flagships? What does successful engagement between a university and community look like, and how is 'success' defined by different parties? Following lines of inquiry such as those of Bose (2015) in the United States and Bank and Sibanda (2018) in South Africa, is there evidence of universities inadvertently reproducing local inequalities and undermining community development through their territorial expansion and other activities?

A recurring theme in this book has been the balancing act of the modern flagship university, enabling it to survive and adapt. History suggests that, even in the face of insolvency, government visitation committees, strikes and new league tables, flagships will continue to survive. But a case can be made for empowering the flagship, providing the financial security to take risks, to take on new research and development projects, and to work with communities in the process. This likely entails a balancing act of a different sort. In 1970, as the developmental university model took root in Africa, a Zambia-based nun wrote to Ernst Stuhlinger, associate director of science at NASA, asking why so much money was being spent on getting a man to the moon when there was such widespread poverty in the United States. His detailed and heartfelt reply acknowledged the dire needs faced by society today, but made the case for balancing these against longer-term investments which may greatly reduce human suffering.

> *Significant progress in the solutions of technical problems is frequently made not by a direct approach, but by first setting a goal of high challenge which offers a strong motivation for innovative work, which fires the imagination and spurs men to expend their best efforts, and which acts as a catalyst by including chains of other reactions. (Ernst Stuhlinger in Mazzucato, 2021, p. 78)*

Flagship universities, in common with their counterparts around the world, are not without their issues and faults. But as potential vehicles for improving the lives of great numbers of people, they are arguably without parallel.

REFERENCES

Acquah, E.H.K. and Budu, J.M. (2017) 'The University of Ghana: A "Premier" University in National Development', in D. Teferra (ed.) *Flagship Universities in Africa*. Cham: Springer International Publishing, pp. 143–195. Available at: https://doi.org/10.1007/978-3-319-49403-6_5.

Acuto, M. (2016) 'Give Cities a Seat at the Top Table', *Nature*, 537(7622), pp. 611–613. Available at: https://doi.org/10.1038/537611a.

Addaney, M. (2018) 'The African Union's Agenda 2063: Education and Its Realization', in A.C. Onuora-Oguno, W.O. Egbewole, and T.E. Kleven (eds) *Education Law, Strategic Policy and Sustainable Development in Africa: Agenda 2063*. Springer International Publishing, pp. 181–197. Available at: https://doi.org/10.1007/978-3-319-53703-0_8.

Addie, J.-P.D. (2016) 'From the Urban University to Universities in Urban Society', *Regional Studies*, 51(7), pp. 1089–1099. Available at: https://doi.org/10.1080/00343404.2016.1224334.

Addie, J.-P.D. (2019a) 'The Limits of University Regionalism', *Urban Geography*, pp. 1–21. Available at: https://doi.org/10.1080/02723638.2019.1591144.

Addie, J.-P.D. (2019b) 'Urban(izing) University Strategic Planning: An Analysis of London and New York City', *Urban Affairs Review*, 55(6), pp. 1612–1645. Available at: https://doi.org/10.1177/1078087417753080.

Addis Ababa University (2020) *A Ten-Year Strategic Plan 2020-2030*. Addis Ababa University Press.

African Centre for Media Excellence (2016) 'Statement: Makerere Visitation Committee Lists Responsibilities', *Uganda Journalists' Resource Centre*. https://ugandajournalistsresourcecentre.com/statement-makerere-visitation-committee-lists-responsibilities/.

AfDB (2024) 'The Ten-Year Strategy African Development Bank Group (2024 – 2033)'. African Development Bank Group. Available at: https://www.afdb.org/en/documents/ten-year-strategy-african-development-bank-group-2024-2033.

African Union Commission (2015) *Agenda 2063: The Africa We Want*. Addis Ababa: African Union Commission.

Aina, T.A. (2010) 'Beyond Reforms: The Politics of Higher Education Transformation in Africa', *African Studies Review*, 53(1), pp. 21–40. Available at: https://doi.org/10.1353/arw.0.0290.

Ajayi, J.F.A. (1996) *The African Experience with Higher Education*. Association of African Universities in association with James Currey and Ohio University Press.

Albrechts, L., Balducci, A. and Hillier, J. (2016) *Situated Practices of Strategic Planning: An international perspective*. Routledge.

Allen, J. and Cochrane, A. (2007) 'Beyond the Territorial Fix: Regional Assemblages, Politics and Power', *Regional Studies*, 41(9), pp. 1161–1175. Available at: https://doi.org/10.1080/00343400701543348.

Amukugo, E.M. (2017) *Democracy and Education in Namibia and Beyond: A Critical Apprasial*. University of Namibia Press.

Anderson, R.D. (1995) *Universities and Elites in Britain Since 1800*. Cambridge University Press.

Aryeetey, E. and Baah-Boateng, W. (2016) *Understanding Ghana's Growth Success Story and Job Creation Challenges*. UNU-WIDER. Available at: https://doi.org/10.35188/UNU-WIDER/2015/029-4.

Asare, S., Mitchell, R. and Rose, P. (2020) 'How Equitable are South-North Partnerships in Education Research? Evidence from sub-Saharan Africa', *Compare: A Journal of Comparative and International Education*, 0(0), pp. 1–20. Available at: https://doi.org/10.1080/03057925.2020.1811638.

Ashwin, P. and Case, J. (2018) *Higher Education Pathways: South African Undergraduate Education and the Public Good*. African Minds. Available at: https://doi.org/10.5281/zenodo.1920793.

Asojo, O.A., Asuzu, M.C. and Adebiyi, A.O. (2014) 'Ibarapa Programme: Half a Century of Rural Health Service, Training, and International Cooperation in Nigeria', *PLoS Neglected Tropical Diseases*, 8(10), p. e3201. Available at: https://doi.org/10.1371/journal.pntd.0003201.

Assié-Lumumba, N.T. (2006) *Higher Education in Africa: Crises, Reforms, and Transformation*. Codesria (Working paper series).

Ayalew, E. (2017) 'Once a Flagship Always a Flagship?: Addis Ababa University in Perspective', in D. Teferra (ed.) *Flagship Universities in Africa*. Springer International Publishing, pp. 91–142. Available at: https://doi.org/10.1007/978-3-319-49403-6_4.

Bank, L., Cloete, N. and van Schalkwyk, F. (eds) (2018) *Anchored in Place: Rethinking the University and Development in South Africa*. African Minds. Available at: https://doi.org/10.47622/9781928331759.

Bank, L. and Sibanda, F. (2018) 'Universities as City-builders: The City-campus Development Opportunity in East London–Buffalo City, South Africa', *Development Southern Africa*, 35(5), pp. 701–715. Available at: https://doi.org/10.1080/0376835X.2018.1502076.

Barrett, A.M. (2013) 'Education and Other Sustainable Development Goals: A shifting Agenda for Comparative Education', *Compare: A Journal of Comparative and International Education*, 43(6), pp. 783–846. Available at: https://doi.org/10.1080/03057925.2013.850285.

Bekele, T.A., Cossa, J. and Barat, S. (2021) 'Toward Building Strategic International University-Society Partnerships in Africa', *Modern Africa: Politics, History and Society*, 9(2), pp. 82–115. Available at: https://doi.org/10.26806/modafr.v9i2.378.

Bekele, T.A. and Ofoyuru, D.T. (2021) 'Emerging University-Society Engagements in Africa: An Analysis of Strategic Plans', *Journal of Comparative & International Higher Education*, 13(1), pp. 151–180. Available at: https://doi.org/10.32674/jcihe.v13i1.1690.

Bekele, T.A., Ofoyuru, D.T. and Woldegiorgis, E.T. (2024) 'Assessing University-Society Engagements: Towards a Methodological Framework', *Innovative Higher Education*, 49(2), pp. 201–221. Available at: https://doi.org/10.1007/s10755-023-09678-1.

Bekker, S.B., Croese, S. and Pieterse, E. (eds) (2021) *Refractions of the National, the Popular and the Global in African Cities*. African Minds.

Birch, E., Perry, D.C. and Taylor, H.L. (2013) 'Universities as Anchor Institutions', *Journal of Higher Education Outreach and Engagement*, 17(3), pp. 7–15.

Bisaso, R. (2017) 'Makerere University as a Flagship Institution: Sustaining the Quest for Relevance', in D. Teferra (ed.) *Flagship Universities in Africa*. Springer International Publishing, pp. 425–466. Available at: https://doi.org/10.1007/978-3-319-49403-6_11.

Bjarnason, S. and Coldstream, P. (eds) (2003). *The Idea of Engagement: Universities in Society*. The Association of Commonwealth Universities.

Bond, P. (2006) 'Global Governance Campaigning and MDGs: From Top-down to Bottom-up Anti-poverty Work', *Third World Quarterly*, 27(2), pp. 339–354. Available at: https://doi.org/10.1080/01436590500432622.

Boni, A. and Walker, M. (2016) *Universities and Global Human Development: Theoretical and Empirical Insights for Social Change*. Routledge. Available at: https://doi.org/10.4324/9781315742793.

Bose, S. (2015) 'Universities and the Redevelopment Politics of the Neoliberal City', *Urban Studies*, 52(14), pp. 2616–2632. Available at: https://doi.org/10.1177/0042098014550950.

Bowen, G.A. (2009) 'Document Analysis as a Qualitative Research Method', *Qualitative Research Journal*, 9(2), pp. 27–40. Available at: https://doi.org/10.3316/QRJ0902027.

Braun, V. and Clarke, V. (2006) 'Using Thematic Analysis in Psychology', *Qualitative Research in Psychology*, 3(2), pp. 77–101. Available at: https://doi.org/10.1191/1478088706qp063oa.

Braun, V. and Clarke, V. (2019) 'Reflecting on Reflexive Thematic Analysis', *Qualitative Research in Sport, Exercise and Health*, 11(4), pp. 589–597. Available at: https://doi.org/10.1080/2159676X.2019.1628806.

British Academy (2021) *Shaping the COVID Decade: Addressing the Long-term Societal Impacts of COVID-19*. The British Academy. Available at: https://doi.org/10.5871/bac19stf/9780856726590.001.

Brown, A. (2022) 'Foreign Direct Investment into Universities: Towards a National Strategy', *HEPI*. https://www.hepi.ac.uk/2022/07/29/foreign-direct-investment-into-universities-towards-a-national-strategy/.

Bryson, J.M., Crosby, B.C. and Bryson, J.K. (2009) 'Understanding Strategic Planning and the Formulation and Implementation of Strategic Plans as a Way of Knowing: The Contributions of Actor-Network Theory', *International Public Management Journal*, 12(2), pp. 172–207. Available at: https://doi.org/10.1080/10967490902873473.

Bunting, I., Cloete, N. and Van Schalkwyk, F. (2013) *An Empirical Overview of Eight Flagship Universities in Africa 2001-2011: A Report of the Higher Education Research and Advocacy Network in Africa (HERANA)*. Centre for Higher Education Transformation.

Cannadine, D.N. (2014) 'Universities 2030: Their Future and Their Funding', *Philanthropy Impact*. https://www.philanthropy-impact.org/article/universities-2030-their-future-and-their-funding.

Cerver Romero, E., Ferreira, J.J.M. and Fernandes, C.I. (2020) 'The Multiple Faces of the Entrepreneurial University: A Review of the Prevailing Theoretical Approaches', *The Journal of Technology Transfer*, 46, pp. 1173–1195. Available at: https://doi.org/10.1007/s10961-020-09815-4.

Chance, S. and Williams, B.T. (2009) 'Assessing University Strategic Plans: A Tool for Consideration', *Educational Planning*, 18(1), pp. 38–54. Available at: https://doi.org/10.21427/D7022N.

Chankseliani, M. and McCowan, T. (2021) 'Higher Education and the Sustainable Development Goals', *Higher Education*, 81(1). Available at: https://doi.org/10.1007/s10734-020-00652-w.

Chankseliani, M., Qoraboyev, I. and Gimranova, D. (2021) 'Higher Education Contributing to Local, National, and Global Development: New Empirical and Conceptual Insights', *Higher Education*, 81(1), pp. 109–127. Available at: https://doi.org/10.1007/s10734-020-00565-8.

Chatterton, P. and Goddard, J. (2000) 'The Response of Higher Education Institutions to Regional Needs', *European Journal of Education*, 35(4), pp. 475–496.

Chaytor, S., Gottlieb, G. and Reid, G. (2021) *Regional Policy and R&D: Evidence, Experiments and Expectations*. 137. HEPI.

Cheater, A.P. (1991) 'The University of Zimbabwe: University, National University, State University, or Party University?', *African Affairs*, 90(359), pp. 189–205. Available at: https://www.jstor.org/stable/722778.

Chigudu, A. and Chavunduka, C. (2020) 'The Tale of Two Capital Cities: The Effects of Urbanisation and Spatial Planning Heritage in Zimbabwe and Zambia', *Urban Forum*, 32. Available at: https://doi.org/10.1007/s12132-020-09410-8.

Chinsembu, G.M.M. and Hamunyela, M. (2015) 'To Integrate or Not: Exploring the Prospects and Challenges of Integrating Indigenous Knowledge at the University of Namibia', in K.C. Chinsembu *et al.* (eds) *Indigenous Knowledge of Namibia*. University of Namibia Press, pp. 361–378. Available at: https://www.jstor.org/stable/j.ctvgc619h.22.

Christopherson, S., Gertler, M. and Gray, M. (2014) 'Universities in Crisis', *Cambridge Journal of Regions, Economy and Society*, 7(2), pp. 209–215. Available at: https://doi.org/10.1093/cjres/rsu006.

Cloete, N. (ed.) (2015) *Knowledge Production and Contradictory Functions in African Higher Education*. African Minds (African higher education dynamics series, 1).

Cloete, N., Bunting, I. and van Schalkwyk, F. (2018) *Research Universities in Africa*. African Minds. Available at: https://doi.org/10.47622/9781928331872.

Cochrane, A. (1998) 'Illusions of Power: Interviewing Local Elites', *Environment and Planning A: Economy and Space*, 30(12), pp. 2121–2132. Available at: https://doi.org/10.1068/a302121.

Cohen, L., Manion, L. and Morrison, K. (2013) *Research Methods in Education*. Seventh Edition. Routledge.

Coleman, J.S. (1986) 'The Idea of the Developmental University', *Minerva*, 24(4), pp. 476–494. Available at: https://www.jstor.org/stable/41820668.

Collinge, C. and Gibney, J. (2010) 'Connecting Place, Policy and Leadership', *Policy Studies*, 31(4), pp. 379–391. Available at: https://doi.org/10.1080/01442871003723259.

Collini, S. (2003) 'HiEdBiz', *London Review of Books*, 25(21).

Compagnucci, L. and Spigarelli, F. (2020) 'The Third Mission of the University: A Systematic Literature Review on Potentials and Constraints', *Technological Forecasting and Social Change*, 161, p. 120284. Available at: https://doi.org/10.1016/j.techfore.2020.120284.

Court, D. (1980) 'The Development Ideal in Higher Education: The Experience of Kenya and Tanzania', *Higher Education*, 9(6), pp. 657–680. Available at: https://doi.org/10.1007/BF02259973.

Cowen, R. (2000) 'Comparing Futures or Comparing Pasts?', *Comparative Education*, 36(3), pp. 333–342. Available at: https://doi.org/10.1080/713656619.

Crowe, T. (2017) Was/Is UCT an Institutionally Colonialist/Sexist/Racist Institution? Part 1 *Tim Crowe's Blog*. http://timguineacrowe.blogspot.com/2017/10/wasis-uct-institutionally.html.

Curtis, S. (ed.) (2014) *The Power of Cities in International Relations*. Routledge (Cities and global governance).

de Sousa Santos, B. (2010) 'The University in the Twenty-first Century', in *The Routledge International Handbook of the Sociology of Education*. Routledge, pp. 274–282.

Dickson, K. (1973) 'The University of Ghana: Aspects of the Idea of an African University', in T.M. Yesufu (ed.) *Creating the African University: Emerging Issues in the 1970's*. Oxford University Press for the Association of African Universities, pp. 102–115.

Douglass, J. (2014) 'Profiling the Flagship University Model: An Exploratory Proposal for Changing the Paradigm from Ranking to Relevancy', *CSHE Research & Occasional Paper Series*, 14(5).

Drori, I. and Honig, B. (2013) 'A Process Model of Internal and External Legitimacy', *Organization Studies*, 34(3), pp. 345–376. Available at: https://doi.org/10.1177/0170840612467153.

Ehlenz, M.M. (2018) 'Defining University Anchor Institution Strategies: Comparing Theory to Practice', *Planning Theory & Practice*, 19(1), pp. 74–92. Available at: https://doi.org/10.1080/14649357.2017.1406980.

Etzkowitz, H. and Dzisah, J. (2008) 'Rethinking Development: Circulation in the Triple Helix', *Technology Analysis & Strategic Management*, 20(6), pp. 653–666. Available at: https://doi.org/10.1080/09537320802426309.

Falqueto, J.M.Z. *et al.* (2020) 'Strategic Planning in Higher Education Institutions: What are the Stakeholders' Roles in the Process?', *Higher Education*, 79(6), pp. 1039–1056. Available at: https://doi.org/10.1007/s10734-019-00455-8.

Farrant, J.H. and Afonso, L.M. (1997) 'Strategic Planning in African Universities: How Relevant Are Northern Models?', *Higher Education Policy*, 10(1), pp. 23–30. Available at: https://doi.org/10.1016/S0952-8733(96)00032-3.

Felde, A.K., Halvorsen, T., Myrtveit, A. and Øygard, R. (2021) *Democracy and the Discourse on Relevance within the Academic Profession at Makerere University.* African Minds. Available at: https://doi.org/10.47622/9781928502272.

Fioreze, C. and McCowan, T. (2018) 'Community Universities in the South of Brazil: Prospects and Challenges of a Model of Non-state Public Higher Education', *Comparative Education*, 54(3), pp. 370–389. Available at: https://doi.org/10.1080/03050068.2018.1433651.

Flanagan, K. *et al.* (2019) *Lessons from the History of UK Science Policy*. British Academy.

Fongwa, S. *et al.* (eds) (2022) *Universities, Society and Development: African Perspectives of University Community Engagement in Secondary Cities*. African Sun Media. Available at: https://doi.org/10.52779/9781991201850.

Frank, D.J. and Meyer, J.W. (2007) 'University Expansion and the Knowledge Society', *Theory and Society*, 36(4), pp. 287–311. Available at: https://doi.org/10.1007/s11186-007-9035-z.

Fredua-Kwarteng, E. (2020) 'Rethinking Strategic Planning in African Universities', *University World News*. https://www.universityworldnews.com/post.php?story=2020100303173555.

Fukuda-Parr, S. (2017) *Millennium Development Goals: Ideas, Interests and Influence*. Routledge. Available at: https://doi.org/10.4324/9781315414232.

Gaffikin, F. and Perry, D.C. (2009) 'Discourses and Strategic Visions: The U.S. Research University as an Institutional Manifestation of Neoliberalism in a Global Era', *American Educational Research Journal*, 46(1), pp. 115–144. Available at: https://doi.org/10.3102/0002831208322180.

Gafu, G. (2019) *The Effects of the Introduction of an Elite Globalised University on Other Institutions: The Case of Kazakhstan*. Doctoral Thesis. UCL (University College London).

Gaidzanwa, R.B. (2020) 'De-Colonising, Indigenising, Diversifying and Making African Universities More Gender-Sensitive: A Case Study of Universities in Zimbabwe', in B. Mpofu and S. Ndlovu-Gatsheni (eds) *The Dynamics of Changing Higher Education in the Global South*. Cambridge Scholars Publishing, pp. 87–102.

Gendron, R.S. (2007) 'Canada's University: Father Levesque, Canadian Aid, and the National University of Rwanda', *Historical Studies*, 73, pp. 63–89.

Gilbert, A.N. (1967) 'Higher Education in Ethiopia', *Africa Today*, 14(2), pp. 6–8. Available at: https://www.jstor.org/stable/4184754.

Giordano, B. (2020) 'Post-Brexit Regional Economic Development Policy in the UK? Some Enduring Lessons from European Union Cohesion Policy', *European Urban and Regional Studies*, p. 0969776420970624. Available at: https://doi.org/10.1177/0969776420970624.

GIZ (2016) 'University Capacity Building Programme (UCBP)'. https://www.giz.de/en/worldwide/18963.html.

Goddard, J. (2009) *Reinventing the Civic University*. 12. Nesta.

Goddard, J. *et al.* (eds) (2016) *The Civic University: The Policy and Leadership Challenges*. Edward Elgar Publishing. Available at: https://doi.org/10.4337/9781784717728.

Goddard, J., Kempton, L. and Vallance, P. (2013) 'The Civic University: Connecting the Global and the Local', in R. Capello, A. Olechnicka, and G. Gorzelak (eds) *Universities, Cities and Regions: Loci for Knowledge and Innovation Creation*. Routledge, pp. 43–63. Available at: https://doi.org/10.4324/9780203097144.

Goodall, L.E. (1970) 'The Urban University: Is There Such a Thing?', *The Journal of Higher Education*, 41(1), pp. 44–54. Available at: https://doi.org/10.2307/1979606.

Goodfellow, T. and Smith, A. (2013) 'From Urban Catastrophe to "Model" City? Politics, Security and Development in Post-conflict Kigali', *Urban Studies*, 50(15), pp. 3185–3202. Available at: https://doi.org/10.1177/0042098013487776.

Gora, P. (2021) 'Has COVID-19 Become a Weapon to Gag Student Activists?', *University World News*. https://www.universityworldnews.com/post.php?story=20210215153817816.

Green, A. (2003) 'Education, Globalisation and the Role of Comparative Research', *London Review of Education*, 1(2). Available at: https://doi.org/10.1080/1474846032000098464.

Grek, S. (2021) 'Researching Education Elites Twenty Years On: Sex, Lies and… Video Meetings', in C. Addey, N. Piattoeva, and J. Law (eds) *Intimate Accounts of Education Policy Research: The Practice of Methods*. Routledge, pp. 16–31. Available at: https://doi.org/10.4324/9781003123613-2.

Guest, M. and Ransom, J. (2020) 'Size Matters: Completing the Jigsaw for Rural and Regional Productivity. Exploring the Concept of Heatmapping for Evidencing the Non-Teaching Interactions and Impact of Smaller and Specialist Universities and Colleges in the United Kingdom', *Journal of Applied Business and Economics*, 22(12). Available at: https://doi.org/10.33423/jabe.v22i12.3883.

Gukurume, S. (2019) 'Surveillance, Spying and Disciplining the University: Deployment of State Security Agents on Campus in Zimbabwe', *Journal of Asian and African Studies*, 54(5), pp. 763–779. Available at: https://doi.org/10.1177/0021909619833414.

Hazelkorn, E. (2007) 'How Do Rankings Impact on Higher Education?', in *OECD Programme on Institutional Management in Higher Education*, (December 2007), pp. 1–2.

Herrschel, T. and Newman, P. (2017) 'Cities Joining States as International Actors', in T. Herrschel and P. Newman (eds) *Cities as International Actors: Urban and Regional Governance Beyond the Nation State*. Palgrave Macmillan UK, pp. 1–22. Available at: https://doi.org/10.1057/978-1-137-39617-4_1.

Hodgkinson, D. (2013) 'The "Hardcore" Student Activist: The Zimbabwe National Students Union (ZINASU), State Violence, and Frustrated Masculinity, 2000–2008', *Journal of Southern African Studies*, 39(4), pp. 863–883. Available at: https://doi.org/10.1080/03057070.2013.858538.

Human Rights Watch (2003) *Lessons in Repression: Violations of Academic Freedom in Ethiopia*. 15(2). Human Rights Watch.

Iddawela, Y., Lee, N. and Rodríguez-Pose, A. (2021) 'Quality of Sub-national Government and Regional Development in Africa', *The Journal of Development Studies*, 57(8), pp. 1282–1302. Available at: https://doi.org/10.1080/00220388.2021.1873286.

Ilie, S. and Rose, P. (2016) 'Is Equal Access to Higher Education in South Asia and sub-Saharan Africa Achievable by 2030?', *Higher Education*, 72(4), pp. 435–455. Available at: https://doi.org/10.1007/s10734-016-0039-3.

Jaganyi, D. *et al.* (2018) *Rwanda: National Urban Policies and City Profiles for Kigali and Huye*. Centre for Sustainable, Healthy, and Learning Communities.

Jansen, J. and Walters, C. (2019) 'The Recent Crisis in South African Universities', *International Higher Education*, (96), pp. 23–24. Available at: https://doi.org/10.6017/ihe.2019.96.10780.

Jessop, B., Brenner, N. and Jones, M. (2008) 'Theorizing Sociospatial Relations', *Environment and Planning D: Society and Space*, 26(3), pp. 389–401. Available at: https://doi.org/10.1068/d9107.

Jhurry, D. (2020) 'Universities to Intensify Efforts to Keep Sustainable Development Goals on Track', *Going Global*. https://www.britishcouncil.org/going-global/blog-posts/university-mauritius-sdgs.

Jiménez-Aceituno, A. *et al.* (2020) 'Local Lens for SDG Implementation: Lessons from Bottom-up Approaches in Africa', *Sustainability Science*, 15(3), pp. 729–743. Available at: https://doi.org/10.1007/s11625-019-00746-0.

Johnson, M.S. (2008) 'Historical Legacies of Soviet Higher Education and the Transformation of Higher Education Systems in Post-Soviet Russia and Eurasia', in D.P. Baker and A. W. Wiseman (eds) *The Worldwide Transformation of Higher Education.* Emerald (MCB UP) (International perspectives on education and society, 9), pp. 159–176. Available at: https://www.emerald.com/insight/content/doi/10.1016/S1479-3679(08)00006-6/full/html.

Jonker, K. and Robinson, B. (2018) 'Integrated Organic Growth: The Cases of Cameroon and Mauritius', in K. Jonker and B. Robinson (eds) *China's Impact on the African Renaissance: The Baobab Grows*. Springer, pp. 217–262. Available at: https://doi.org/10.1007/978-981-13-0179-7_9.

Kajela, A. (2022) 'Revisiting African Higher Education in Line with the Ideals of Pan-Africanism: Bringing Agenda 2063 Aspirations to the Forefront'. *Proceedings of the 20th International Conference on Private Higher Education in Africa*, April 27-28. Available at: https://doi.org/10.2139/ssrn.4658475.

Kamola, I. (2014) 'The African University as "Global" University', *PS: Political Science & Politics*, 47(03), pp. 604–607. Available at: https://doi.org/10.1017/S1049096514000705.

Kariwo, M.T. (2013) 'Higher Education in Zimbabwe: From Crisis to Reconstruction', in E. Shizha (ed.) *Restoring the Educational Dream. Rethinking Educational Transformation in Zimbabwe*. Africa Institute of South Africa, pp. 216–233.

Kassahun, M. (2021) 'The Governance of Addis Ababa Light Rail Transit', in S. Bekker, S. Croese and E. Pieterse (eds) *Refractions of the National, the Popular and the Global in African Cities*. African Minds, pp. 149–172. Available at: https://doi.org/10.47622/9781928502159_11.

Kaweesi, M., Bisaso, R. and Ezati, B.A. (2019) 'The Nature of and Motive for Academic Research in Higher Education: A sub-Saharan African Perspective', *International Journal of African Higher Education*, 6(1), pp. 1–25. Available at: https://doi.org/10.6017/ijahe.v6i1.10577.

Key, S. (1996) 'Economics or Education: The Establishment of American Land-Grant Universities', *The Journal of Higher Education*, 67(2), pp. 196–220. Available at: https://doi.org/10.1080/00221546.1996.11780256.

Kigotho, W. (2020) 'Makerere Plans New Approach to HE, Will Others Follow?', *University World News*. https://www.universityworldnews.com/post.php?story=20200930150900613.

Kiraka, R. *et al.* (2020) 'University League Tables and Ranking Systems in Africa: Emerging Prospects, Challenges and Opportunities', in E. Mogaji, F. Maringe, and R. Ebo Hinson (eds) *Understanding the Higher Education Market in Africa*. Routledge, pp. 199–214. Available at: https://doi.org/10.4324/9780429325816.

Kirby-Harris, R. (2003) 'Universities Responding to Policy: Organisational Change at the University of Namibia', *Higher Education*, 45(3), pp. 353–374. Available at: https://doi.org/10.1023/A:1022656720659.

Kithome, D. (2019) 'Africa and the Sustainable Development Goals: Are the SDGs and Agenda 2063 Complementary policies?' *African Organisation for Standardisation ARSO*.

Kraemer-Mbula, E. *et al.* (eds) (2019) *Transforming Research Excellence: New Ideas from the Global South*. African Minds. Available at: https://doi.org/10.47622/9781928502067.

Kragelund, P. and Hampwaye, G. (2015) 'The Confucius Institute at the University of Zambia: A New Direction in the Internationalisation of African Higher Education?', in H.K. Adriansen, L.M. Madsen, and S. Jensen (eds) *Higher Education and Capacity Building in Africa: The Geography and Power of Knowledge Under Changing Conditions*. Routledge, pp. 101–122. Available at: https://doi.org/10.4324/9781315734620.

Krippendorff, K. (2010) 'Content Analysis', in N. Salkind (ed.) *Encyclopedia of Research Design*. SAGE Publications, Inc., pp. 233–238. Available at: https://doi.org/10.4135/9781412961288.

Kuzhabekova, A., Soltanbekova, A. and Almukhambetova, A. (2018) 'Educational Flagships as Brokers in International Policy Transfer: Learning from the Experience of Kazakhstan', *European Education*, 50(4), pp. 353–370. Available at: https://doi.org/10.1080/10564934.2017.1365306.

Lahtinen, A. (2015) 'China's Soft Power: Challenges of Confucianism and Confucius Institutes', *Journal of Comparative Asian Development*, 14(2), pp. 200–226. Available at: https://doi.org/10.1080/15339114.2015.1059055.

Latapí Agudelo, M.A., Jóhannsdóttir, L. and Davídsdóttir, B. (2019) 'A Literature Review of the History and Evolution of Corporate Social Responsibility', *International Journal of Corporate Social Responsibility*, 4(1), pp. 1–23. Available at: https://doi.org/10.1186/s40991-018-0039-y.

Lebeau, Y. (2008) 'Universities and Social Transformation in sub-Saharan Africa: Global Rhetoric and Local Contradictions', *Compare: A Journal of Comparative and International Education*, 38(2), pp. 139–153. Available at: https://doi.org/10.1080/03057920701676905.

Lebeau, Y. (2020) 'Field of Higher Education Research, Africa', in P.N. Teixeira and J.C. Shin (eds) *The International Encyclopedia of Higher Education Systems and Institutions*. Springer Netherlands, pp. 444–450. Available at: https://doi.org/10.1007/978-94-017-8905-9_190.

Lee, N. (2019) 'Inclusive Growth in Cities: A Sympathetic Critique', *Regional Studies*, 53(3), pp. 424–434. Available at: https://doi.org/10.1080/00343404.2018.1476753.

Lee, N. (2020) 'Inclusive Innovation as Urban Policy: A Review and Critique', *LSE*. https://personal.lse.ac.uk/leen/Inclusive_Innovation_DRAFT.pdf.

Lemarchand, G., A. and Susan, S. (2014) *Mapping Research and Innovation in the Republic of Zimbabwe*. UNESCO.

Leresche, K. (2021) 'Trends and Innovation Impacting Capacity to Deliver on the African Agenda 2063', *RUFORUM Triennial Thought Pieces* [Preprint], (4).

Levinson, R.M. (1989) 'The Faculty and Institutional Isomorphism', *Academe*, 75(1), pp. 23–27. Available at: https://doi.org/10.2307/40249781.

Li Kam Wah, H. (2017) 'The University of Mauritius: Overview of a Flagship University in a Small Island State', in D. Teferra (ed.) *Flagship Universities in Africa*. Springer International Publishing, pp. 241–279. Available at: https://doi.org/10.1007/978-3-319-49403-6_7.

Lim, M.A. (2018) 'The Building of Weak Expertise: The Work of Global University Rankers', *Higher Education*, 75(3), pp. 415–430. Available at: https://doi.org/10.1007/s10734-017-0147-8.

Livsey, T. (2017) *Nigeria's University Age: Reframing Decolonisation and Development*. Palgrave Macmillan (Cambridge Imperial and Post-Colonial Studies). Available at: https://doi.org/10.1057/978-1-137-56505-1.

Lucci, P. et al. (2016) *Projecting Progress: Are Cities on Track to Achieve the SDGs by 2030?* Overseas Development Institute.

MacGregor, K. (2014) 'A New University, New International Leader, New Future', *University World News*. https://www.universityworldnews.com/post.php?story=20140620093600774.

MacKinnon, D. et al. (2021) 'Reframing Urban and Regional "Development" for "Left Behind Places"', *Cambridge Journal of Regions, Economy and Society*, 15(1), pp. 39–56. Available at: https://doi.org/10.1093/cjres/rsab034.

Makerere University (2008) *Strategic Plan 2008/09-2018/19*. Makerere University.

Makerere University (2020) *Makerere University Strategic Plan 2020-2030: Unlocking the Knowledge Hub in the Heart of Africa*. Makerere University.

Mamdani, M. (2007) *Scholars in the Marketplace: The Dilemmas of Neo-Liberal Reform at Makerere University, 1989-2005*. CODESRIA (Council for the Development of Social Science Research in Africa).

Mamdani, M. (2008) 'Higher Education, the State and the Marketplace', *Journal of Higher Education in Africa / Revue de l'enseignement supérieur en Afrique*, 6(1), pp. 1–10. Available at: https://www.jstor.org/stable/jhigheducafri.6.1.1.

Mamdani, M. (2018) 'The African University', *London Review of Books*, 40(14), pp. 29–32.

Manirakiza, V. et al. (2019) 'City Profile: Kigali, Rwanda', *Environment and Urbanization ASIA*, 10(2), pp. 290–307. Available at: https://doi.org/10.1177/0975425319867485.

Marginson, S. (2016) *The Dream Is Over: The Crisis of Clark Kerr's California Idea of Higher Education*. University of California Press. Available at: https://doi.org/10.1525/luminos.17.

Marginson, S. (2022) 'Space and Scale in Higher Education: The Glonacal Agency Heuristic Revisited', *Higher Education*, 84(6), pp. 1365–1395. Available at: https://doi.org/10.1007/s10734-022-00955-0.

Marginson, S. and Rhoades, G. (2002) 'Beyond National States, Markets, and Systems of Higher Education: A Glonacal Agency Heuristic', *Higher Education*, 43, pp. 281–309. Available at: https://doi.org/10.1023/A:1014699605875.

Markusen, A. (1999) 'Fuzzy Concepts, Scanty Evidence, Policy Distance: The Case for Rigour and Policy Relevance in Critical Regional Studies', *Regional Studies*, 33(9), pp. 869–884. Available at: https://doi.org/10.1080/00343409950075506.

Martin, L. and Ibbotson, P. (2019) 'Boundary Spanning as Identity Work in University Business Engagement Roles', *Studies in Higher Education*, pp. 1–13. Available at: https://doi.org/10.1080/03075079.2019.1688281.

Martinez, R., Bunnell, T. and Acuto, M. (2020) 'Productive Tensions? The "City" Across Geographies of Planetary Urbanization and the Urban Age', *Urban Geography*, pp. 1–12. Available at: https://doi.org/10.1080/0272363 8.2020.1835128.

Masaiti, G. and Mwale, N. (2017) 'University of Zambia: Contextualization and Contribution to Flagship Status in Zambia', in D. Teferra (ed.) *Flagship Universities in Africa*. Springer International Publishing, pp. 467–505. Available at: https://doi.org/10.1007/978-3-319-49403-6_12.

Masaiti, G. and Mwale, N. (2020) 'The Drive and Nature of Internationalisation of Higher Education in Zambia', *International Journal of African Higher Education*, 7(2), pp. 99–121. Available at: https://doi.org/10.6017/ ijahe.v7i2.12899.

Mastop, H. and Faludi, A. (1997) 'Evaluation of Strategic Plans: The Performance Principle', *Environment and Planning B: Planning and Design*, 24(6), pp. 815–832. Available at: https://doi.org/10.1068/b240815.

Materu, P., Obanya, P. and Righetti, P. (2011) 'The Rise, Fall, and Reemergence of the University of Ibadan, Nigeria', in P.G. Altbach and J. Salmi (eds) *The Road to Academic Excellence: The Making of World-Class Research Universities*. World Bank Publications, pp. 195–228.

Mau, S. (2019) *The Metric Society: On the Quantification of the Social*. John Wiley & Sons.

Mazzucato, M. (2021) *Mission Economy: A Moonshot Guide to Changing Capitalism*. Penguin UK.

Mbah, M., Johnson, A.T. and Chipindi, F.M. (2021) 'Institutionalizing the Intangible through Research and Engagement: Indigenous Knowledge and Higher Education for Sustainable Development in Zambia', *International Journal of Educational Development*, 82. Available at: https://doi.org/10.1016/j.ijedudev.2021. 102355.

Mbonyinshuti, J. d'Amour (2021a) 'Indigenous Knowledge Institute Aspires to Global Mandate', *University World News*. https://www.universityworldnews.com/post.php?story=2021100614485245.

Mbonyinshuti, J. d'Amour (2021b) 'Universities Have a Role in Rwanda's Reconciliation', *University World News*. https://www.universityworldnews.com/post.php?story=20210504134133841.

McCowan, T. (2016) 'Universities and the Post-2015 Development Agenda: An Analytical Framework', *Higher Education*, 72(4), pp. 505–523. Available at: https://doi.org/10.1007/s10734-016-0035-7.

McCowan, T. (2018) 'Five Perils of the Impact Agenda in Higher Education', *London Review of Education*, 16(2), pp. 279–295. Available at: https://doi.org/10.18546/LRE.16.2.08.

McCowan, T. (2019) *Higher Education for and beyond the Sustainable Development Goals*. Palgrave Macmillan (Palgrave Studies in Global Higher Education). Available at: https://link.springer.com/book/10.1007/978-3-030-19597-7.

McCowan, T. (2020) *The Impact of Universities on Climate Change: A Theoretical Framework*. Working Paper 1. Climate-U Transforming Universities for a Changing Climate.

Mcdowell, G.R. (2003) 'Engaged Universities: Lessons from the Land-Grant Universities and Extension', *The ANNALS of the American Academy of Political and Social Science*, 585(1), pp. 31–50. Available at: https:// doi.org/10.1177/0002716202238565.

Mejía-Dugand, S., Croese, S. and Reddy, S.A. (2020) 'SDG Implementation at the Local Level: Lessons From Responses to the Coronavirus Crisis in Three Cities in the Global South', *Frontiers in Sustainable Cities*, 2, pp. 1–6. Available at: https://doi.org/10.3389/frsc.2020.598516.

Melhuish, C. (2015) 'The Role of the University in Urban Regeneration', *Architectural Research Quarterly*, 19(1), pp. 5–8. Available at: https://doi.org/10.1017/S1359135515000299.

Ministry of Education Rwanda (2019) 'Higher Learning Institutions'. https://www.mineduc.gov.rw/higher-learning-institutions.

Mohamedbhai, G. (2014) 'Massification in Higher Education Institutions in Africa: Causes, Consequences and Responses', *International Journal of African Higher Education*, 1(1), pp. 59–83. Available at: https://doi. org/10.6017/ijahe.v1i1.5644.

Mohamedbhai, G. (2021) 'Professor Walter Kamba: A Man of Conscience', *University World News*. https:// www.universityworldnews.com/post.php?story=20210915110915828.

Molebatsi, P. (2022) 'Place, Public Good and Higher Education in South Africa', *Journal of Higher Education in Africa / Revue de l'enseignement supérieur en Afrique*, 20(2), pp. 159–184. Available at: https://www.jstor.org/stable/48719831.

Moreira da Silva, J. and Kamal-Chaoui, L. (2019) 'Helping Cities and Regions Achieve the SDGs: Partnering for Decentralised Development Co-operation', *Development Matters (OECD)*. https://oecd-development-matters.org/2019/12/09/helping-cities-and-regions-achieve-the-sdgs-partnering-for-decentralised-development-co-operation/.

Mtawa, N.N. (2019) *Human Development and Community Engagement through Service-Learning: The Capability Approach and Public Good in Education*. Palgrave Macmillan Cham. Available at: https://link.springer.com/book/10.1007/978-3-030-34728-4.

Mtawa, N.N. and Wangenge-Ouma, G. (2021) 'Questioning Private Good Driven University-Community Engagement: A Tanzanian Case Study', *Higher Education*, 83, pp. 597–611. Available at: https://link.springer.com/article/10.1007/s10734-021-00685-9.

Mumba, L. (2021) 'Vice Chancellor's State of the University of Zambia Address: Wednesday, 17th March 2021'. Confucius Multi-Purpose Hall, University of Zambia.

Mupeta, S. *et al.* (2020) 'Civic Entrepreneurship: The Implementation of Civic Innovations in the Governance of the University of Zambia', *Advances in Social Sciences Research Journal*, 7(7), pp. 674–685. Available at: https://doi.org/10.14738/assrj.77.8670.

Mutero, I.T. (2021) 'Partnership Dynamics in University-Community Engagement: A Case Study of the TibaSA Multi-Disciplinary Research Team in uMkhanyakude District, KwaZulu-Natal, South Africa', *International Journal of African Higher Education*, 8(1), pp. 117–138. Available at: https://doi.org/10.6017/ijahe.v8i1.13373.

Mutisya, E. (2018) 'Shaping Prosperity by 2030: The Role of Universities in Africa's Socio- Economic Transformation', *CESDEV Issue Paper* [Preprint], (2018/5).

Nabaho, L. *et al.* (2022) 'The Third Mission of Universities on the African Continent: Conceptualisation and Operationalisation', *Higher Learning Research Communications*, 12(1), pp. 81–98. Available at: https://doi.org/10.18870/hlrc.v12i1.1298.

Naidoo, R. (2011) 'Rethinking Development: Higher Education and the New Imperialism', in R. King, S. Marginson, and R. Naidoo (eds) *Handbook on Globalization and Higher Education*. Edward Elgar, pp. 40–58. Available at: https://doi.org/10.4337/9780857936233.00012.

National Universities Commission (2024) Nigerian Universities. https://www.nuc.edu.ng/?s=Nigerian+Universities.

Ndlovu-Gatsheni, S.J. (2017) 'The Emergence and Trajectories of Struggles for an 'African University': The Case of Unfinished Business of African Epistemic Decolonisation', *Kronos*, 43(1), pp. 51–77. Available at: http://dx.doi.org/10.17159/2309-9585/2017/v43a4.

Nega, M. (2018) 'Reflections on the Trimmed Roles of Research Institutes at Addis Ababa University', *The Ethiopian Journal of Higher Education*, 5(1), pp. 1–29.

Nelles, J. and Vorley, T. (2010) 'From Policy to Practice: Engaging and Embedding the Third Mission in Contemporary Universities', *International Journal of Sociology and Social Policy*, 30(7/8), pp. 341–353. Available at: https://doi.org/10.1108/01443331011060706.

Ngwana, T. (2003) 'University Strategic Planning in Cameroon: What Lessons for sub-Saharan Africa?', *Education Policy Analysis Archive*, 11(47).

Nóvoa, A. and Yariv-Mashal, T. (2003) 'Comparative Research in Education: A Mode of Governance or a Historical Journey?', *Comparative Education*, 39(4), pp. 423–438. Available at: https://doi.org/10.1080/0305006032000162002.

NSS (2020) 'About Us Ghana National Service Scheme', *National Service Scheme*. https://nss.gov.gh/about-us/.

Ntsebeza, L. (2020) 'The Ebb and Flow of the Fortunes of African Studies at the University of Cape Town: An Overview', *Social Dynamics*, 46(2), pp. 356–372. Available at: https://doi.org/10.1080/02533952.2020.1815335.

NYSC (2020) 'NYSC - About Scheme'. https://www.nysc.gov.ng/aboutscheme.html.

OECD (ed.) (2007) *Higher Education and Regions: Globally Competitive, Locally Engaged*. OECD Publishing. Available at: https://doi.org/10.1787/9789264034150-en.

Okebukola, P.A. (2015) *Higher Education and Africa's Future: Doing What is Right*. Covenant University.

Oketch, M. (2014) 'Human Capital Theory and Educational Policy Strategies in sub-Saharan Africa: A Retrospective Overview', *International Journal of Educational Development in Africa*, 1(1), pp. 96–107. Available at: https://doi.org/10.25159/2312-3540/48.

Oketch, M. (2016) 'Financing Higher Education in sub-Saharan Africa: Some Reflections and Implications for Sustainable Development', *Higher Education*, 72, pp. 525–539. Available at: https://doi.org/10.1007/s10734-016-0044-6.

Olayinka, A.I. (2015) *Agenda for the Accelerated Development of the University of Ibadan through Consolidation and Innovation, 2015-2020*. Ibadan University Press.

Olayinka, A.I. (2020) *My Stewardship as Vice-Chancellor (2015-2020): Partial Listing of Fundamental Achievements*. https://www.ui.edu.ng/news/my-stewardship-vice-chancellor-2015-2020

Oldekop, J.A. *et al.* (2020) 'COVID-19 and the Case for Global Development', *World Development*, 134, pp. 1–4. Available at: https://doi.org/10.1016/j.worlddev.2020.105044.

Onwuemele, A. (2018) 'University-Community Engagement in Nigeria: Evidence from Selected Universities', *Mediterranean Journal of Social Sciences*, 9(5). Available at: https://doi.org/10.2478/mjss-2018-0136.

Owens, T.L. (2017) 'Higher Education in the Sustainable Development Goals Framework', *European Journal of Education*, 52(4), pp. 414–420. Available at: https://doi.org/10.1111/ejed.12237.

Paasi, A. and Metzger, J. (2017) 'Foregrounding the Region', *Regional Studies*, 51(1), pp. 19–30. Available at: https://doi.org/10.1080/00343404.2016.1239818.

Parnell, S. and Pieterse, E. (2014) *Africa's Urban Revolution*. Bloomsbury Academic. Available at: https://doi.org/10.5040/9781350218246.

Peil, M. (1997) 'The African Experience with Higher Education', *African Affairs*, 96(382), pp. 123–124. Available at: https://doi.org/10.1093/oxfordjournals.afraf.a007800.

Petersen, I., Kruss, G. and van Rheede, N. (2022) 'Strengthening the University Third Mission through Building Community Capabilities Alongside University Capabilities', *Science and Public Policy*, 49(6), pp. 890–904. Available at: https://doi.org/10.1093/scipol/scac036.

Phillips, H. (2004) 'A Caledonian College in Cape Town and Beyond: An Investigation into the Foundation(s) of the South African University System', *South African Journal of Higher Education*, 17(3), pp. 122–128. Available at: https://doi.org/10.4314/sajhe.v17i3.25411.

Phoenix, D. (2021) 'The Gradual Reshaping of the Education Sector', *HEPI*. https://www.hepi.ac.uk/2021/02/24/the-gradual-reshaping-of-the-education-sector/.

Pike, A., Rodríguez-Pose, A. and Tomaney, J. (2007) 'What Kind of Local and Regional Development and for Whom?', *Regional Studies*, 41(9), pp. 1253–1269. Available at: https://doi.org/10.1080/00343400701543355.

Pike, A., Rodríguez-Pose, A. and Tomaney, J. (2017) 'Shifting Horizons in Local and Regional Development', *Regional Studies*, 51(1), pp. 46–57. Available at: https://doi.org/10.1080/00343404.2016.1158802.

Porter, M.E. and Kramer, M.R. (2011) 'Creating Shared Value', *Harvard Business Review*, 2011(January-February).

Powell, J.J.W., Baker, D.P. and Fernandez, F. (2017) *The Century of Science: The Global Triumph of the Research University*. Emerald Group Publishing.

Prysor, D. and Henley, A. (2018) 'Boundary Spanning in Higher Education Leadership: Identifying Boundaries and Practices in a British University', *Studies in Higher Education*, 43(12), pp. 2210–2225. Available at: https://doi.org/10.1080/03075079.2017.1318364.

Psacharopoulos, G. (1981) 'Returns to Education: An Updated International Comparison', *Comparative Education*, 17(3), pp. 321–341. Available at: https://doi.org/10.1080/0305006810170308.

Pugh, R. *et al.* (2016) 'A Step into the Unknown: Universities and the Governance of Regional Economic Development', *European Planning Studies*, 24(7), pp. 1357–1373. Available at: https://doi.org/10.1080/09654313.2016.1173201.

Ramtohul, R. (2012) 'Academic Freedom in a State-Sponsored African University: The Case of the University of Mauritius', *Journal of Academic Freedom*, 3, pp. 1–21.

Ranking Web of Universities (2022) 'Sub-Saharan Africa Ranking (July 2022 edition 2022.2.beta)'. https://www.webometrics.info/en/Ranking_africa/Sub_saharan_Africa.

Ransom, J. (2023) *A 'Local Turn' for Africa's Flagship Universities? A Comparative Case Study of the University of Rwanda and Universities in Nine African City Regions*. Doctoral thesis. UCL (University College London).

Regmi, K.D. (2015) 'Can Lifelong Learning Be the Post-2015 Agenda for the Least Developed Countries?', *International Journal of Lifelong Education*, 34(5), pp. 551–568. Available at: https://doi.org/10.1080/02601 370.2015.1070209.

Rickards, L. *et al.* (2016) 'Urban Studies After the Age of the City', *Urban Studies*, 53(8), pp. 1523–1541. Available at: https://doi.org/10.1177/0042098016640640.

Rwendeire, A. (2017) *'Bringing the Future to the Present': The Report of the Visitation Committee on Makerere University, 2016.* Government of the Republic of Uganda.

Sánchez-Barrioluengo, M. and Benneworth, P. (2019) 'Is the Entrepreneurial University Also Regionally Engaged? Analysing the Influence of University's Structural Configuration on Third Mission Performance', *Technological Forecasting and Social Change*, 141, pp. 206–218. Available at: https://doi.org/10.1016/j. techfore.2018.10.017.

Sanderson, M. (ed.) (2016) *The Universities in the Nineteenth Century.* Taylor & Francis. Available at: https://doi. org/10.4324/9781315443881.

Sayed, Y. and Sprague, T. (2013) 'Editorial: Post-2015 Education and Development: Contestation, Contradictions and Consensus', *Compare: A Journal of Comparative and International Education*, 43(6), pp. 783–846. Available at: https://doi.org/10.1080/03057925.2013.850285.

Schwarz, S.M. (1957) 'Review of Soviet Professional Manpower: Its Education, Training, and Supply', *The Russian Review*, 16(2), pp. 66–68. Available at: https://doi.org/10.2307/126125.

SCImago (2022) 'Research and Innovation Rankings - Africa 2022'. https://www.scimagoir.com/rankings. php?country=Africa.

Serafini, P.G. *et al.* (2022) 'Sustainable Development Goals in Higher Education Institutions: A Systematic Literature Review', *Journal of Cleaner Production*, 370. Available at: https://doi.org/10.1016/j.jclepro.2022.133473.

Shaketange, L., Kanyimba, A.T. and Brown, E. (2017) 'The Challenges and Measures for Internship among Fourth-Year Students in the Department of Lifelong Learning and Community Education at the University of Namibia', *Creative Education*, 08(14), p. 2258–2274. Available at: https://doi.org/10.4236/ce.2017.814155.

Shizha, E. and Kariwo, M.T. (2012) *Education and Development in Zimbabwe: A Social, Political and Economic Analysis.* Sense Publishers.

Shumba, A. and Mawere, D. (2012) 'The Causes and Impact of the Brain Drain in Institutions of Higher Learning in Zimbabwe', *International Migration*, 50(4), pp. 107–123. Available at: https://doi.org/10.1111/j.1468-2435.2012.00749.x.

Siegfried, J.J., Sanderson, A.R. and McHenry, P. (2007) 'The Economic Impact of Colleges and Universities', *Economics of Education Review*, 26(5), pp. 546–558. Available at: https://doi.org/doi.org/10.1016/j. econedurev.2006.07.010.

Simon, N. (2020) 'Vision 2030: The World Is Changing, Are We?' *University of Cape Town News.* http://www. news.uct.ac.za/article/-2020-08-17-vision-2030-the-world-is-changing-are-we.

Smit, W. (2018) 'Urban Governance in Africa: An Overview', in C. Ammann and T. Förster (eds) *African Cities and the Development Conundrum.* The Graduate Institute Geneva (International Development Policy), pp. 55–77.

Smith, A. (2013) 'Education, Equity and Social Cohesion: The Contribution of Education to Peacebuilding in the Post-2015 Development Goals', *Compare: A Journal of Comparative and International Education*, 43(6), pp. 783–846. Available at: https://doi.org/10.1080/03057925.2013.850285.

Söderström, O., Paasche, T. and Klauser, F. (2014) 'Smart Cities as Corporate Storytelling', *City*, 18(3), pp. 307–320. Available at: https://doi.org/10.1080/13604813.2014.906716.

Soudien, C. (2013) 'What's Being Overlooked in the Post-2015 Agenda for Education?', *Compare: A Journal of Comparative and International Education*, 43(6), pp. 783–846. Available at: https://doi.org/10.1080/030579 25.2013.850285.

Ssembatya, V.A. (2020) 'Sustaining Research Excellence and Productivity with Funding from Development Partners: The Case of Makerere University', in E. Kraemer-Mbula, R. Tijssen, M. L. Wallace, and R. McLean (eds) *Transforming Research Excellence: New Ideas from the Global South.* African Minds. Available at: https://doi.org/10.5281/zenodo.3603928.

Stensaker, B. *et al.* (2019) 'Stratified University Strategies: The Shaping of Institutional Legitimacy in a Global Perspective', *The Journal of Higher Education*, 90(4), pp. 539–562. Available at: https://doi.org/10.1080/00 221546.2018.1513306.

Stubbs, R., Dickson, N. and Husbands, C. (2020) *Levelling Up Yorkshire and Humber: Health as the New Wealth post COVID*. Yorkshire & Humber Academic Health Science Network, the NHS Confederation and Yorkshire Universities.

Swedberg, R. (2018) 'How to Use Max Weber's Ideal Type in Sociological Analysis', *Journal of Classical Sociology*, 18(3), pp. 181–196. Available at: https://doi.org/10.1177/1468795X17743643.

Talloires Network (2024) 'Talloires Network of Engaged Universities Signatory Members', *Talloires Network of Engaged Universities*. https://talloiresnetwork.tufts.edu/who-we-are/talloires-network-members/.

Tamrat, W. (2019) 'Re-engaging with Community Service in Universities', *University World News*. https://www.universityworldnews.com/post.php?story=20190501082547889.

Tamrat, W. (2020) 'What Next for a Partially Differentiated HE System?', *University World News*. https://www.universityworldnews.com/post.php?story=20200929080901365.

Teferra, D. (2016) 'African Flagship Universities: Their Neglected Contributions', *Higher Education*, 72, pp. 79–99. Available at: https://doi.org/10.1007/s10734-015-9939-x.

Teferra, D. (ed.) (2017) *Flagship Universities in Africa*. Palgrave Macmillan. Available at: https://doi.org/10.1007/978-3-319-49403-6.

Teferra, D. (2020) 'The Irrelevance of the Re-Configured Definition of Internationalisation to the Global South: Intention Versus Coercion', *International Journal of African Higher Education*, 7(2). Available at: https://doi.org/10.6017/ijahe.v7i2.12905.

Teichler, U. (1996) 'Comparative Higher Education: Potentials and Limits', *Higher Education*, 32, pp. 431–465. Available at: https://doi.org/10.1007/BF00133257.

The New Times (2012) 'Education Minister Wants One Varsity Bill Expedited', *The New Times*. https://www.newtimes.co.rw/article/82079/National/education-minister-wants-one-varsity-bill-expedited.

The University for Development Studies (UDS). (2024). About Uds. https://www.uds.edu.gh/about/.

Thrift, N. (2022) 'Why Do UK Universities Have No Vision for Their Future?', *Times Higher Education (THE)*. https://www.timeshighereducation.com/blog/why-do-uk-universities-have-no-vision-their-future.

Tight, M. (2012) *Researching Higher Education*. McGraw-Hill Education.

Tikly, L. (2019) 'Education for Sustainable Development in the Postcolonial World: Towards a Transformative Agenda', in I. Clemens, S. Hornberg, and M. Rieckmann (eds) *Bildung und Erziehung im Kontext globaler Transformationen*. First Edition. Verlag Barbara Budrich, pp. 17–78. Available at: https://doi.org/10.2307/j.ctvm201r8.5.

Times Higher Education (2023) 'World University Rankings 2023', *Times Higher Education (THE)*. https://www.timeshighereducation.com/world-university-rankings/2023/world-ranking.

Trippl, M., Smith, H.L. and Sinozic, T. (2012) 'The 'Third Mission' of Universities and the Region: Comparing the UK, Sweden and Austria', *Paper to be presented at the 52nd European Congress of the RSAI 21st August - 25th August 2012, Bratislava, Slovakia* [Preprint].

Twiringiyimana, R., Daniels, C. and Chataway, J. (2021) 'STI Policy and Governance in Sub-Saharan Africa: Fostering Actors' Interactions in Research and Innovation', *Industry and Higher Education*, 35(5), pp. 553–624. Available at: https://doi.org/10.1177/09504222211026218.

UCT (2016) *Distinguishing UCT: A Strategic Planning Framework for 2016-2020*. University of Cape Town.

UCT (2020a) 'History Introduction'. http://www.uct.ac.za/main/about/history.

UCT (2020b) 'Master Historian Reflects on UCT's History'. http://www.news.uct.ac.za/article/-2020-02-14-master-historian-reflects-on-ucts-history.

UCT (2021a) *Annual Report for 2020*. University of Cape Town.

UCT (2021b) *Vision 2030: Unleash Human Potential for a Fair and Just Society*. University of Cape Town.

Udegbe, B. and Ekhaguere, G.O.S. (2017) 'University of Ibadan: A Beacon of Higher Education in Africa', in D. Teferra (ed.) *Flagship Universities in Africa*. Springer International Publishing, pp. 281–332. Available at: https://doi.org/10.1007/978-3-319-49403-6_8.

Ufomba, H.U. (2020) 'The African Union Development Agenda 2063: Can Africa Get It Right?', *Brazilian Journal of Development*, 6(8), pp. 62626–62648. Available at: https://doi.org/10.34117/bjdv6n8-627.

UN (2015) *Transforming Our World: The 2030 Agenda for Sustainable Development*. United Nations. Available at: https://doi.org/10.1891/9780826190123.ap02.

UN (2022a) *The Sustainable Development Goals Report 2022*. United Nations.

UN (2022b) 'UNSD — Methodology'. https://unstats.un.org/unsd/methodology/m49/.

UN (2023) *Quality Education: The Sustainable Development Goals Extended Report 2022*. United Nations.

UNESCO (1963) *The Development of Higher Education in Africa: Report of the Conference on the Development of Higher Education in Africa, Tananarive, 3-12 September 1962*. UNESCO.

UNESCO (2016) *TVET, Higher Education and Innovation Policy Review: Namibia*. United Nations Education, Scientific and Cultural Organization.

University of Ghana (2014) *Strategic Plan 2014-2024*. University of Ghana.

University of Mauritius (2015) *Strategic Plan 2015-2020*. University of Mauritius.

University of Namibia (2019) *Strategic Plan 2019-2024*. University of Namibia.

University of Rwanda (2018a) *Facts and Figures 2013 - 2018*. University of Rwanda.

University of Rwanda (2018b) *University of Rwanda 2018-2025 Strategic Plan*. University of Rwanda.

University of Zambia (2016) 'History of UNZA'. https://www.unza.zm/international/?p=history.

University of Zambia (2018) *Strategic Plan 2018-2022*. University of Zambia.

University of Zimbabwe (2019a) *2019-2025 Strategic Plan: Educating to Change Lives*. University of Zimbabwe.

University of Zimbabwe (2019b) 'Chairman of Council Statement'. https://www.uz.ac.zw/index.php/statement-chairman.

University of Zimbabwe (2019c) 'Foreword by Minister'. https://www.uz.ac.zw/index.php/minister-foreword.

University of Zimbabwe (2019d) 'Vice Chancellor's Statement'. https://www.uz.ac.zw/index.php/vice-chancellor-statement.

Unterhalter, E. and Howell, C. (2021) 'Unaligned Connections or Enlarging Engagements? Tertiary Education in Developing Countries and the Implementation of the SDGs', *Higher Education*, 81, pp. 9–29. Available at: https://doi.org/10.1007/s10734-020-00651-x.

Unterhalter, E., Peppin Vaughan, R. and Smail, A. (2013) 'Secondary and Higher Education in the Post-2015 Framework', *Compare: A Journal of Comparative and International Education*, 43(6), pp. 783–846. Available at: https://doi.org/10.1080/03057925.2013.850285.

Vaira, M. (2004) 'Globalization and Higher Education Organizational Change: A Framework for Analysis', *Higher Education*, 48, pp. 483–510. Available at: https://doi.org/10.1023/B:HIGH.0000046711.31908.e5.

Vale, L.J. (2014) 'The Politics of Resilient Cities: Whose Resilience and Whose City?', *Building Research & Information*, 42(2), pp. 191–201. Available at: https://doi.org/10.1080/09613218.2014.850602.

van Schalkwyk, F. and de Lange, G. (2018) 'The Engaged University and the Specificity of Place: The Case of Nelson Mandela Metropolitan University', *Development Southern Africa*, 35(5), pp. 641–656. Available at: https://doi.org/10.1080/0376835X.2017.1419858.

Wandira, A. (1981) 'University and Community: Evolving Perceptions of the African University', *Higher Education*, 10(3), pp. 253–273. Available at: https://doi.org/10.1007/BF00139560.

Watson, D. *et al.* (2011) *The Engaged University: International Perspectives on Civic Engagement*. Taylor & Francis.

Watson, V. (2019) 'The Return of the City-region in the New Urban Agenda: Is this Relevant in the Global South?', *Regional Studies*, 55(1), pp. 19–28. Available at: https://doi.org/10.1080/00343404.2019.1664734.

Westen, G. van *et al.* (2021) 'Introduction to the Handbook of Translocal Development and Global Mobilities', in A. Zoomers *et al.* (eds) *Handbook of Translocal Development and Global Mobilities*. Edward Elgar Publishing, pp. 1–11. Available at: https://doi.org/10.4337/9781788117425.00007.

White, B.J. (1998) *Relevance, Rhetoric and Reality: National Development at the University of Namibia*. 73. Centre for African Studies at Edinburgh University.

Wirtu, D. (2020) 'Interdisciplinary Thematic Research at Addis Ababa University: Challenges and Opportunities', *The Ethiopian Journal of Education*, 40(1), pp. 43–63.

Wodajo, M. (1973) 'Haile Selassie I University: A Brief Profile', in T.M. Yesufu (ed.) *Creating the African University: Emerging Issues in the 1970's*. Oxford University Press for the Association of African Universities, pp. 244–250.

Woldegiyorgis, A.A., Tamrat, W. and Teferra, D. (2022) 'Unpacking "Relevance" in North South Collaboration', *International Higher Education*, (112), pp. 7–9.

World Bank (2019a) 'Population, Total - Namibia, Rwanda Data'. https://data.worldbank.org/indicator/SP.POP.TOTL?locations=NA-RW.

World Bank (2019b) 'World Bank Open Data: Services, Value Added (% of GDP)'. https://data.worldbank.org/indicator/NV.SRV.TOTL.ZS.

Wrong, M. (2021) *Do Not Disturb: The Story of a Political Murder and an African Regime Gone Bad*. HarperCollins.

Yesufu, T.M. (ed.) (1973) *Creating the African University: Emerging Issues in the 1970's*. Oxford University Press for the Association of African Universities.

Zapp, M. and Ramirez, F.O. (2019) 'Beyond Internationalisation and Isomorphism: The Construction of a Global Higher Education Regime', *Comparative Education*, 55(4), pp. 473–493. Available at: https://doi.org/10.1080/03050068.2019.1638103.

Zavale, N.C. and Schneijderberg, C. (2022) 'Mapping the Field of Research on African Higher Education: A Review of 6483 Publications from 1980 to 2019', *Higher Education*, 83, pp. 199–233. Available at: https://doi.org/10.1007/s10734-020-00649-5.

Zulu, J.M. *et al.* (2019) 'The Challenge of Community Engagement and Informed Consent in Rural Zambia: An Example from a Pilot Study', *BMC Medical Ethics*, 20(45). Available at: https://doi.org/10.1186/s12910-019-0382-x.

ABOUT THE AUTHOR

Dr James Ransom is a higher education researcher whose work looks at how universities can help solve challenges facing society. He is an honorary senior research fellow at UCL Faculty of Education and Society, director of Open Impact, and a specialist advisor on higher education to the European Bank for Reconstruction and Development. He is also head of research at the National Centre for Entrepreneurship in Education (NCEE) in the UK. From 2020 to 2022 he was a research affiliate at the University of Rwanda.

www.ingramcontent.com/pod-product-compliance
Lightning Source LLC
Chambersburg PA
CBHW080555270326
41929CB00019B/3323